100 Backgammon Puzzles

PAUL LAMFORD

THE LYONS PRESS

Copyright © 1999 by Paul Lamford

First Lyons Press Edition, 2001

Originally published in 1999 by Chameleon Books,
an imprint of André Deutsch, Ltd., UK.

Typeset by Games and Pastimes Consultancy

Printed in the United States of America

10 9 8 7 6 5 4 3 2 1

Library of Congress Cataloging-in-Publication Data is available on file.

ISBN 1-58574-209-0

Contents

Acknowledgements

The author would like to thank Simon Gasquoine and Miranda Moore for invaluable assistance in checking all the material in this book and for proofreading and editing the text. Shaun Herd, Alistair Hogg, Fintan O'Boyle, Sue Perks and Mick Vacarey also assisted in proofreading and testing the positions. However the author takes full responsibility for any errors and would welcome comments sent to him at gampas@aol.com.

To Sue

Introduction

Backgammon is played on a board with 24 points and the starting

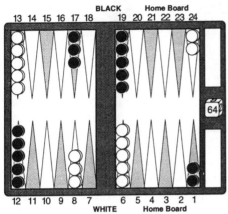

position is as shown in the diagram.

White moves anti-clockwise with his home board at the bottom right and Black moves clock-wise with his home board at the top right. By agreement the colours or direction may be reversed.

Moves are always indicated from the point of view of the player moving and are shown by indicating the point of departure, followed by an oblique, followed by the point of arrival.

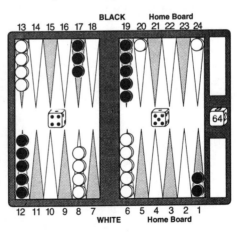

The game starts with each player rolling one die in the half of the board on the player's right. Let us say that White rolls a five and Black rolls a four. The player who rolls the higher number takes the roll - if both players roll the same they roll again.

White decides to move one checker from his 13-point to his eight-point and one checker from his 24-point to his 20-point. The move is notated 13/8 24/20 and leads to the position above.

Notation for hits

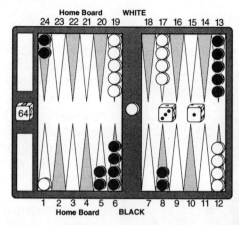

After the opening roll, each player in turn rolls two dice in the half of the board on his right. Let us say that Black replies with a roll of 3-1 which he has played as shown.

Black has moved one man from his eight-point, hitting the White checker on his five-point, and one man from his six-point, to cover the man on his five-point. This move is notated as 8/5* 6/5. The asterisk is used to show that a checker has been hit and that checker is placed on the bar which is the dividing area between the two halves of the board. In this book all other diagrams are shown from White's point of view, but the above diagram may help you visualise the notation for Black's moves.

Doubles and Entering from the Bar

When a double is rolled, four separate moves are played and one could notate them separately. However, it is usual when two men are moved from one point to another to indicate this by placing "(2)" after the move.

Here White has replied with 1-1, and he entered from the

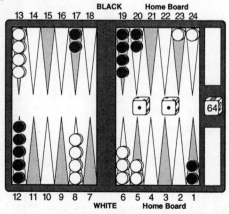

bar with one man, moved it on to the 23-point and made his five-point with the other two aces. This move is notated b/23 6/5(2). The "b" is used to indicate that the departure point was the bar. If the same man continues to move, as here, where the actual move was b/24 24/23, the move is notated with just the point of departure and the point of arrival. As White moved two men from the six-point to the five-point, this is shown by the "(2)" after the move 6/5.

Bearing off

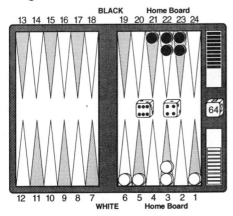

When all the men have reached the home board, checkers may be borne off with a roll of a die corresponding to a point on which a checker is located, or, when there is no checker on that point or any higher point, a checker may be borne off the highest point on which there is a checker. In the diagram above White has rolled a 6-4 and he decides to play the four first (which he is allowed to do) and moves a checker from the six-point to the two-point. With the six, he bears a man off from the five-point. The rule is that both numbers on the dice must be played if possible, or if only one can be played legally, then the higher number must be played. Provided this rule is followed, either number may be played first. When notating a move, the move that is played first is shown first. So here White's move would be notated 6/2 5/o. The "o" indicates that a man is being moved from the five-point off the board, into the storage tray shown on the right.

The Cube

Even social players will have seen a cube with the numbers 2, 4, 8, 16, 32 and 64 on its faces. It is sometimes wrongly assumed that this is only used when playing for money, but the cube is a vital part of the game and is also used in tournament play throughout the world. At the start of the game it is placed at the edge of the board between the two players with the face displaying 64 uppermost. This indicates that the cube has not yet been offered during the current game. Some cubes are available with the number one instead of the number 64, and are less confusing to a beginner.

Doubling and Redoubling

At any point during the game, but only prior to rolling, a player may make an initial double by turning the cube so that the face showing "2" is uppermost and offering it to the opponent by placing it in the middle of the board. The opponent can accept the cube on two, often referred to as "taking", when it is placed on his side of the board, or reject the cube, often called "dropping" or "passing". If he accepts, the game continues with the cube on two and this means that the winner scores twice the number of points achieved in the game. If he rejects the cube, one point is scored by the person doubling. After the initial double, only the person on whose side the cube is situated may redouble to four, again prior to rolling, and the opponent again has the option of accepting or rejecting. If he rejects, then he concedes two points. If he accepts the game is played for four times the number of points scored in the game. An initial double may be made by either player, but subsequent redoubles may only be made by the player on whose side of the board the cube is located, and the strategy for redoubling is somewhat different from that for making an initial double.

Gammons and Backgammons

If a player bears off all his checkers before the opponent bears off any checkers, but the loser has no men in the winner's home board or on the bar, then the game is scored at twice the value of the cube for the winner and this is known as a "gammon". If a player bears off all his checkers before the opponent has borne off any checkers, and the loser still has one or more men in the winner's home board or on the bar, then the game is scored at treble the value of the cube for the winner. This, a rare outcome, is known as a "backgammon".

Basic Strategy

There are two types of backgammon, money games and tournament match-play. Although the basic principles are similar, the strategy can be significantly different.

General
The object of backgammon is, in essence, to bear off all your checkers before your opponent, but it is rare that both sets of checkers race around the board without one or more of them being hit and sent to the bar. Sometimes you have to take risks which increase your chances of winning the game. The basic strategy in the early stages is to build blocking points which restrain your

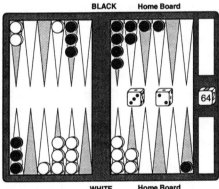

opponent and at the same time to prevent your own men being blocked in. Take the following position:

Although White can safety the loose blot on the 16-point with 16/13, and safety the blot on the 10-point with 10/8, this would be poor play. The correct move is to make the bar-point with 10/7 9/7. Making a prime, which is the term used for the resulting blockade of five points in a row, is one of the main aims of backgammon. Black will need to roll a three and then a six to escape his back man.

The Doubling Cube
The correct strategy in using the doubling cube is the key to success in backgammon. Errors made in accepting a cube wrongly or in not doubling are the most costly . The basic rule is that you accept a cube when you win at least one time in four. This seems strange to a beginner who tends to think you should only accept the cube when you are favourite. The following position helps to clarify this:

The basic principle of deciding whether to accept a double is to compare the risk with the reward. If you pass then you are –1. If you take and lose you are –2. If you take and win you are +2. So you risk one point to gain three. Therefore if you are winning at least one quarter of the time you

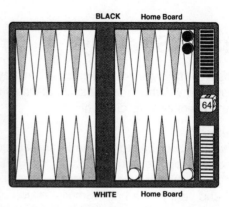

should accept. Here White has 23 winning rolls and 13 losing rolls. White should double and Black should accept. In 36 games Black will lose 46 points and win 20 for an average loss of $^{26}/_{36}$ points per game. This is less than the one point he would lose by passing, so he should accept. Of course in the one game Black cannot lose a fraction of a point, but over the long-term he will gain by accepting.

A guide to doubling and accepting – PRAT(!)
This stands for Position, Race and Threats and is a useful guide for deciding when to double and when to accept. A good rule-of-

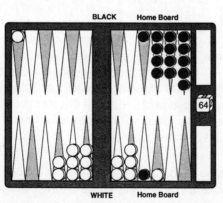

thumb for beginners is that to double you need an advantage in two of these three areas. If you have a clear advantage in all three then your opponent should pass. In the position opposite White has a five-prime in front of Black's checker, an advantage in position, and he threatens to

point on that checker, making a six-prime, but Black is way ahead in the race– if he escapes he will win. So White should double and Black should accept.

The Race

When all contact has been broken, so that it is impossible to hit any

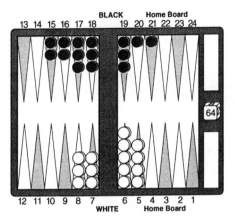

further checkers, the game becomes a race, and the player who rolls the higher numbers will win if the starting position is equal. The decision when to double in such positions may be worked out very accurately but to calculate it you need to do what is known as a pip-count. You add the total numbers of pips each side needs to bear off all their checkers.

Take the position opposite: White's pip-count is arrived at by counting the totals of the points on which each man is located, so here that is [(3x8)+(3x7)+(5x6)+(4x5)] = 95. Black's pip-count is arrived at the same way, but looking at the board from Black's point of view, so that is [(2x10)+(2x9)+(3x8)+(3x7)+(3x6)+5+4] = 110. A general rule for doubling is if the lead is more than 10% of the leader's pip count he should double; if it is more than 12% the trailer should pass. The lead is 15 which is about 16% of 95, so Black should pass.

Duplication and Diversification

One of the most important aspects of moving checkers is to minimise the number of good rolls for your opponent. In this position you have rolled a poor roll, 6-1, and you should play 22/16 10/9. This duplicates fours for your opponent, in that

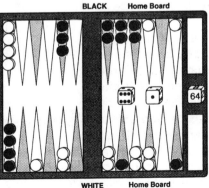

he may hit either the man on your nine-point or your 16-point, or he could make an anchor with 24/20. You hope he does not roll a four, and there will be fewer good things he can do with his other numbers.

Diversification is somewhat different. Here you are trying to give yourself as many good numbers as possible next roll. The position

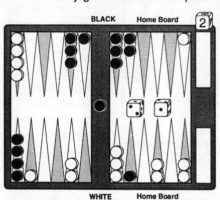

opposite is what is called a blitz, where White is attacking and trying to close out one or more black checkers. White should play 6/5*11/9. This diversifies the good numbers on White's next roll, giving him fours to cover the blot on the five-point and sixes to hit on Black's bar-point. In addition the man on the nine-point can hit with a five if Black enters on White's four-point.

Market Losers

When you have a threat which, if you execute it, will cause your opponent not to accept

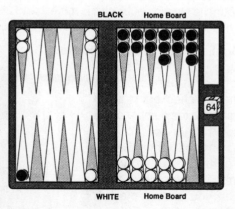

the cube, you are said to have market losers. In the position opposite if White rolls an ace or a six he will "lose his market". White is a favourite to hit so he should double the stakes now. If White misses, Black should immediately redouble to four and White should pass, but the initial double is still correct because White loses his market on all the 24 numbers that hit – two-thirds of his rolls.

Types of game

We have mentioned races, where there is no contact, and blitzes, an example of which is shown in the last diagram. Other types of game include back games, where a player has two or more anchors in the opponent's board, prime versus prime, where each player has a five-point prime or greater with one or more checkers trapped behind it and holding games, where each side has a point which he may clear at a later stage.

Money Play

In a money game, there is obviously no match score to consider. If you lose four points in one game, you forget about it and play the next game from scratch. If you have won or lost 20 points in the evening, that should have no effect on your decisions in the next game. However, one major difference between money play and tournament play is the rule about gammons:

The Jacoby Rule

In games played for money, gammons and backgammons only count as single wins if an initial double has not been made. The effect is that a player should double the stakes earlier to ensure that any gammon or backgammon he achieves is rewarded with the appropriate multiple.

Tournament Play

Matches in tournaments are very different from money games. Firstly there is usually a fixed entry fee to a tournament and the risk is therefore clearly defined. In an evening of playing money games, a player may win or lose 50 or 100 points at stakes which vary from £1 per point or less to £5,000 per point in some exclusive clubs. A match in a tournament is played until one player reaches a set number of points, with 11 being a common number in British events. There is no difference between winning 11-10 and winning 11-0; the sole object is to be first past the post. Consequently, if you are leading 9-0 and your opponent has doubled you to two, you would never redouble to four in a match to 11 points. In a money game, however, the previous gains or losses are irrelevant and each game is a separate entity. In tournaments, the Jacoby Rule does not apply, and you can win a gammon or backgammon without doubling. You always have to consider the match score. For example, if your opponent doubles you to two when you are trailing 7-9 in a match to 11 points, if you accept the cube, you must redouble to four before your next roll, however bad your position. As explained, the margin of victory is of no significance.

The Crawford Rule

While there is no Jacoby Rule in tournament play, there is another rule which is **only** used in tournaments, called the Crawford Rule. As soon as one player reaches a score one point from victory (so in a 11-point match, as soon as one player reaches 10 points) the cube may not be used by either player in the next game only. This game is known as the Crawford game and its purpose is to give some advantage to a player leading, say, 10-9. Without it, the trailer would double immediately. After the Crawford game, the trailer can, and should, double immediately in all subsequent games.

Different checker plays at money play and tournament play

You are solely trying to maximise your winnings in a money game. This means that gammons are always worth winning. In a tournament game, however, there is no point winning a gammon if you don't need it. If you are playing a money game in the diagrammed position, you would hit the black blot with 8/7* and continue with 7/4. Putting the black checker on the bar gives you an excellent chance of a gammon. After Black enters he still has a number of men in the outfield which will need to be brought home. However, if the score were 9-9 in a tournament match of the first to 11 points, the correct play would be 8/5 2/1, breaking all contact with Black. The chance of Black winning the race is tiny (under 1%), but if you do hit, Black may remain on the bar for a while and hit a shot as you bear-off and go on to win. Black is about five times more likely to win if you hit him.

Basic Probabilities

As a mathematical game, backgammon and probability theory are inextricably linked, but there is no need for a great knowledge of mathematics to play the game well. However some basic knowledge of probability is needed and some useful percentages that the reader should know are as follows:

Probability of hitting a direct shot (to the nearest percentage)

Pips from target	Probability
1	31%
2	33%
3	39%
4	42%
5	42%
6	47%

As can be seen you are always an underdog to hit a direct shot.

Probability of hitting an indirect shot

Pips from target	Probability
7	17%
8	17%
9	14%
10	8%
11	6%
12	8%
15,16 or 18	3%

Probability of entering from the bar against different boards

Points made in board	Probability
1	97%
2	89%
3	75%
4	56%
5	31%
6	0%

Probability of winning certain types of positions

One man closed out but your other men in your board – 5%

A closed board against a man on the bar when your opponent has borne off 14 checkers – 8%

A closed board when your opponent has borne off 10 checkers – 25%

A closed board when your opponent has borne off 5 checkers – 75%

Chances of being gammoned in certain positions

One man closed out and your other men in your board – 5%

Two men closed out and your other men in your board – 45%

Three men closed out and your other men in your board – 90%

Approximate chances at different scores in a 5-point match

0-0 50%	0-1 42%	0-2 34%	0-3 25%	0-4 15%
1-0 58%	1-1 50%	1-2 41%	1-3 32%	1-4 17%
2-0 66%	2-1 59%	2-2 50%	2-3 40%	2-4 25%
3-0 75%	3-1 68%	3-2 60%	3-3 50%	3-4 30%
4-0 85%	4-1 83%	4-2 75%	4-3 70%	4-4 50%

These figures assume each player is of the same ability and take into account the Crawford Rule which prevents a player from doubling in the game after one player reaches a score one point from victory.

How to use this book.

The 100 positions in this book are divided into 50 checker plays and 50 cube decisions. Write down your choice before looking at the solution on the next page, and if you wish compare your score with the rating chart on page 128. A hint is provided with each puzzle, but if you read the hint first, then only score half a mark for a correct answer. The puzzles become progressively harder in each section. In each position the location of the cube is shown on the right-hand side of the board and should be noted. A few positions are termed Double Match Point, which means that both players need one point for victory, and the cube is not shown as neither player can use it. In all cases it is White to play.

Part One:
Checker Plays

1

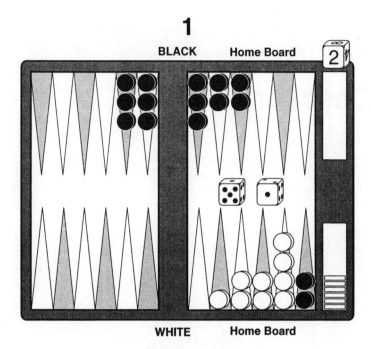

Money Game
White to play 5-1

HINT
Make sure you have established all the
legal plays in the position

Solutions to all puzzles are given on the following page

2

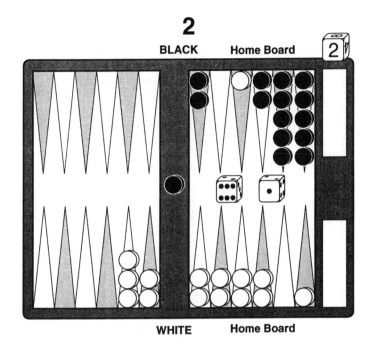

Money Game
White to play 6-1

HINT
**Black is stuck behind a six-prime;
what is the best way to exploit this?**

Solutions to all puzzles are given on the following page

3

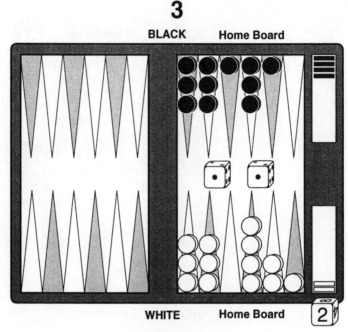

BLACK   **Home Board**

WHITE   **Home Board**

Money Game
White to play 1-1

Solution to Puzzle 1

The correct move is the little trick 5/4 4/o. As long as you play both numbers on the dice, you can play them in either order and you are not obliged to bear off whenever you can.

TIP: IN THE BEAR-OFF LOOK OUT FOR PLAYING THE SMALLER NUMBER FIRST — IT CAN BE TO YOUR ADVANTAGE

4

BLACK   Home Board

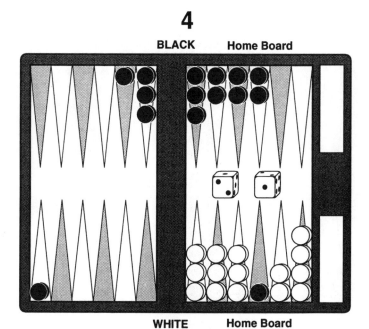

WHITE   Home Board

Double Match Point
White to play a 2-1

Solution to Puzzle 2

The correct play is 21/20 8/2, volunteering a double shot. The point is that Black cannot escape after hitting and White has good chances of picking up a second man when Black is forced to move off his six-point with most of his re-entry numbers.

TIP: WHEN YOU HAVE TRAPPED A MAN BEHIND A SIX-PRIME YOU SHOULD BE TRYING TO PICK UP A SECOND MAN

5

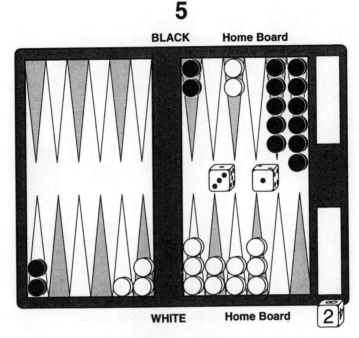

Money Game
White to play 3-1

HINT
Black is likely to leave a shot in the near future;
what is the best way to prepare for that?

Solution to Puzzle 3

White should take two men off with three of the aces with 1/o 2/o.
The last ace should be played 5/4 to fill the gap on the four-point,
otherwise any future fours will have to be moved from the six-point
or five-point.

> TIP: THE BASIC RULE IN THE BEAR-OFF IS TO TAKE MEN
> OFF IF YOU CAN; OTHERWISE FILL THE HIGHEST GAP

6

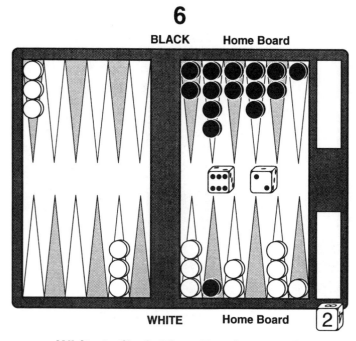

BLACK Home Board

WHITE Home Board

White trails 0-1 in a 5-point match
White to play 6-2

HINT
When you take a risk consider both the
gains and the losses

Solution to Puzzle 4

The right move is to take two men off with 2/o 1/o. A play such as 4/3* 3/1 is reasonable but the longer Black hangs around the better chance he has of hitting a shot. The weakest play is 5/3* 4/3, making a closed board but very likely to leave a shot next time.

TIP: AVOID LEAVING AN ODD MAN ON THE OUTSIDE POINT UNLESS THE POINT NEXT TO IT ALSO HAS AN ODD MAN

7

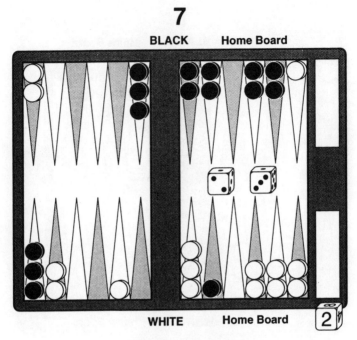

Money Game
White to play 3-2

HINT
Doing two things is often better than doing one

Solution to Puzzle 5

White should split the men on the 21-point with 21/20 and then play 8/5 with the three. He is quite likely to get a double shot when Black is forced to break next turn from his mid-point. Even if Black rolls a seven, White will get more shots with his split men.

TIP: WHEN THE OPPONENT HAS A CRUSHED BOARD LOOK
TO SPLIT AN ANCHOR TO MAXIMISE HITTING CHANCES

8

BLACK   **Home Board**

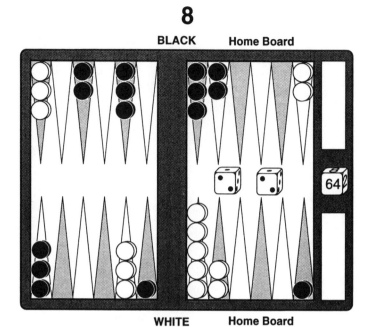

WHITE   **Home Board**

Money Game
White to play 2-2

HINT
When you roll a double try to do something on both sides of the board if possible

---

Solution to Puzzle 6

The correct play is to play safe with 8/2 6/4. If you hit with 13/5*, it is true that you will win more games, but if Black hits back you are in danger of losing a gammon and with it the match.

TIP: WHEN YOUR OPPONENT HAS THE STRONGER BOARD
ONLY HIT WHEN THERE IS NO REASONABLE ALTERNATIVE

9

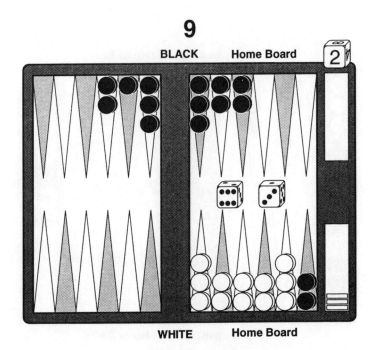

Money Game
White to play 6-3

HINT
White has to leave a shot with this roll;
where is the best place to leave it?

Solution to Puzzle 7

The correct play is 24/21 8/6. This accomplishes two vital tasks at once: it prepares the escape of the back man and safeties White's blot. Hitting with 8/5* 13/11 is great if Black doesn't enter, but very bad if he does. A similar drawback applies to 8/5* 5/3.

TIP: IF YOU WANT TO HIT, CONSIDER BOTH THE UPSIDE
AND DOWNSIDE AND WEIGH THEM AGAINST EACH OTHER

10

BLACK Home Board

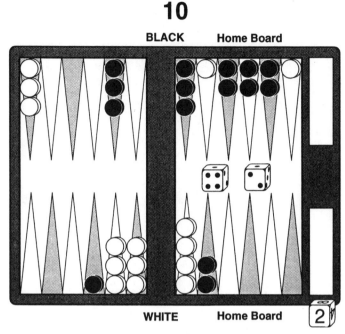

WHITE Home Board

Money Game
White to play 4-2

Solution to Puzzle 8

The right play is to make two points with 24/22(2) 6/4(2). White thus strengthens his forward position and secures a better anchor. If Black does not roll a six next turn, White will be well-placed. Hitting with 13/7* 7/5 does not make maximum use of a good roll.

TIP: MAKING TWO GOOD POINTS IS NEARLY ALWAYS BETTER THAN HITTING

11

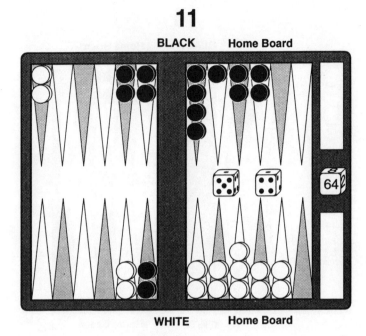

Money Game
White to play 5-4

HINT
White is ahead in the race here;
what does that suggest?

Solution to Puzzle 9

The correct play is 6/o 6/3 leaving the blot on the six-point. Although White could take two men off with 6/o 3/o, this is of no consequence if Black hits as Black will usually win by redoubling to four. By leaving the blot on the outside, White is less likely to blot next time.

TIP: DO NOT LEAVE A BLOT ON AN INNER-BOARD POINT UNLESS YOU HAVE TAKEN OFF MORE THAN SEVEN MEN

12

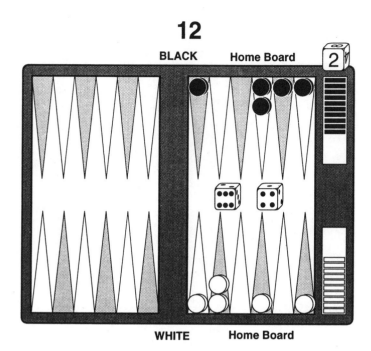

BLACK   Home Board

WHITE   Home Board

Money Game
White to play 6-4

HINT
There are two plays to consider here;
why is one of them correct?

Solution to Puzzle 10

The correct play is 24/20 6/4. To hit here is much too dangerous; Black will have no difficulty entering and he will attack on his five-point if he can. Making the "golden anchor" is correct and then White should start his board by slotting the four-point.

TIP: USUALLY MAKE THE "GOLDEN ANCHOR" OR THE "GOLDEN POINT" IN PREFERENCE TO HITTING A BLOT

13

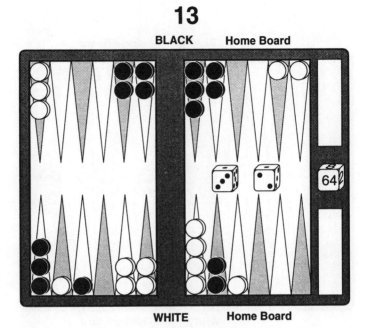

BLACK   Home Board

WHITE   Home Board

Money Game
White to play 3-2

HINT
White can hit and cover here, but is that best?

Solution to Puzzle 11

It is correct here to play 13/9 13/8. If Black does not get a deuce,
White will double and Black will have to pass unless he has rolled
a large double. Because Black has a blot in board, now is the time
to make the run to safety.

**TIP: YOU SHOULD LEAVE A SHOT WHEN YOU THEN HAVE A
STRONG DOUBLE IF YOU ARE MISSED**

14

BLACK   Home Board

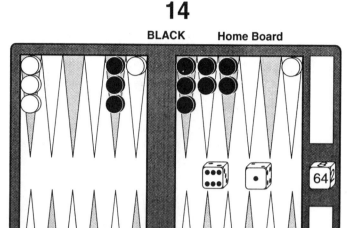

WHITE   Home Board

Money Game
White to play 6-1

HINT
**White has a choice of several points to make
with this roll; which one is best?**

Solution to Puzzle 12

The correct move is to play the four first with 6/2 and to bear a man off with 5/o. This ensures that White will bear off two men next turn unless he rolls 4-1, 4-2, 4-3 or 2-2. If White plays 6/o 5/1, the two gaps could prove costly.

TIP: SOMETIMES IT IS CORRECT TO WASTE A PIP IN THE
BEAR-OFF IF YOU THUS REDUCE THE NUMBER OF GAPS

15

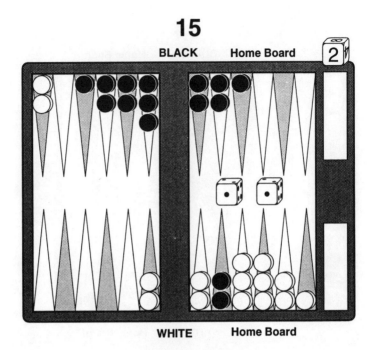

Money Game
White to play 1-1

HINT
**White's main aim is not to leave a future shot;
what move achieves this goal?**

Solution to Puzzle 13

The correct play is to make an anchor with 24/21 23/21. Even if Black hits the man on the 11-point White will then have a good defensive position. The alternatives leave shots without any great gain because of Black's high anchor.

**TIP: GETTING AN ANCHOR AT THE EDGE OF A PRIME IS
USUALLY BETTER THAN HITTING A SHOT**

16

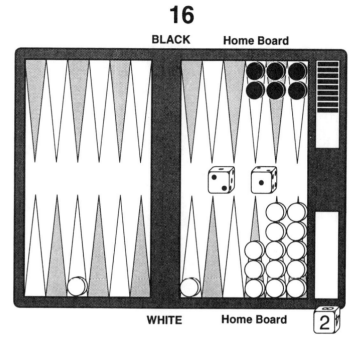

WHITE   Home Board

Money Game
White to play 2-1

> **HINT**
> **White should save the gammon here,**
> **but care is needed**

Solution to Puzzle 14

The right play is 24/18 11/10. White then leaves no shots and stops Black from attacking on his bar-point. The alternatives of making the five-point or bar-point give Black too much leeway. Hitting two men with 8/2*/1* is wrong here because Black has a strong board.

TIP: PREFER TO MAKE AN ANCHOR RATHER THAN A BLOCKING POINT IF YOU TIDY UP BLOTS AT THE SAME TIME

17

BLACK   Home Board

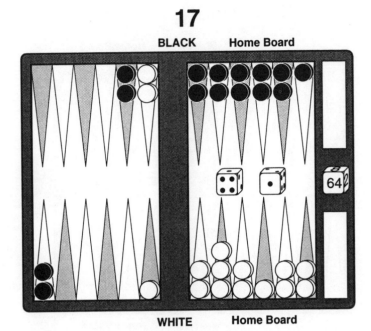

WHITE   Home Board

Money Game
White to play 4-1

Solution to Puzzle 15
The correct play is 13/12(2) 7/6(2). It is useful to move both checkers to the 12-point from which all sixes can move to safety, but wrong to continue to the 11-point because you may leave a later direct shot. 7/6(2) clears the bar-point which has to be done at some time.

TIP: WHEN YOU ARE AHEAD IN THE RACE AVOID MAKING A NEW POINT WHICH IS "SIX AWAY" FROM AN ANCHOR

18

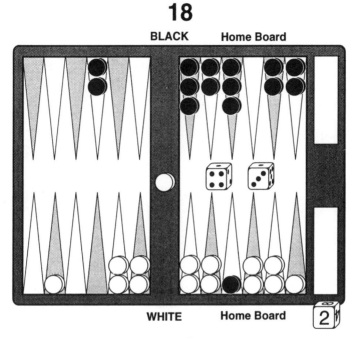

Money Game
White to play 4-3

HINT
The three is forced; you can hit with 8/4*, pick up a
blot with 11/7 or run out with 22/18

Solution to Puzzle 16

The right play is 10/8 6/5 which guarantees saving the gammon
next turn. Other moves leave at least one roll that doesn't work; for
example, 10/7 would fail to get off the gammon next turn with a roll
of 5-4.

TIP: WHEN YOU ARE A BIG FAVOURITE TO SAVE THE
GAMMON LOOK OUT FOR SURPRISING ROLLS THAT FAIL

19

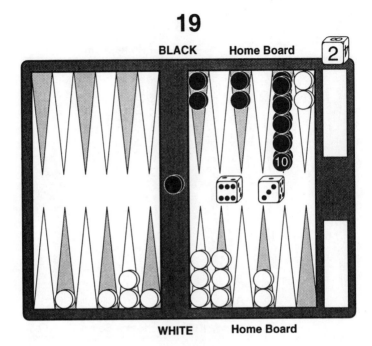

Money Game
White to play 6-3

HINT
Your first priority is to attack and contain the black
checker when it enters from the bar

Solution to Puzzle 17

The right play is 5/1 4/3, preserving a five-point board with one
point slotted, but more importantly keeping a spare six so that White
does not have to break the 18-point anchor next roll. This increases
the chances that Black will have to leave a shot before White.

TIP: IN ANY "MUTUAL HOLDING GAME", SUCH AS THIS,
TRY TO RETAIN A SPARE SIX IF POSSIBLE

20

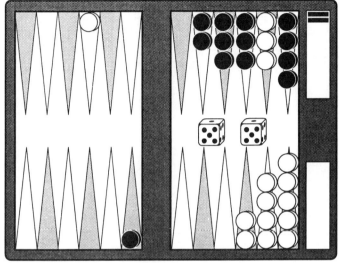

BLACK Home Board

WHITE Home Board

Double Match Point
White to play 5-5

HINT
**Try to maximise contact when you have a bad position
and are not worried about losing a gammon**

Solution to Puzzle 18

The correct play in this situation is to hit with 8/4*. Although your opponent will hit you back with all ones and fours, if he stays on the bar you will gain substantially. The other plays still leave many shots but the gain when the opponent misses does not compensate.

TIP: WHEN YOU OWN THE CUBE, YOU DO NOT HAVE TO
FEAR YOUR OPPONENT USING IT NEXT TURN

21

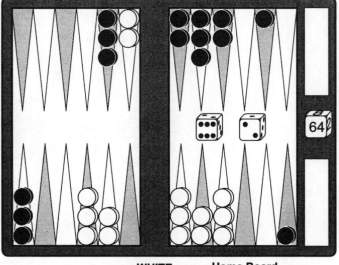

**Money Game
White to play 6-2**

**HINT
White is trying to contain the checker on his ace-point.
What move best serves this purpose?**

Solution to Puzzle 19

Although it leaves several blots, the correct play is to make the
two-point with 8/2 5/2. If Black does not enter you will then be
favourite to make the four-point or the seven-point next turn, while
if Black does hit, his board is weak and you may hit a shot later.

**TIP: WHEN YOUR OPPONENT IS ON THE BAR GIVE
PRIORITY TO MAKING A NEW INNER-BOARD POINT**

22

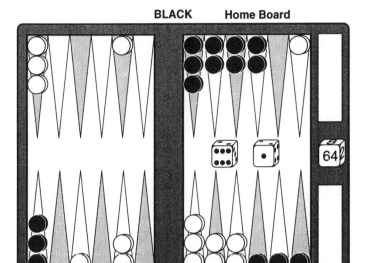

BLACK   Home Board

WHITE   Home Board

Money Game
White to play 6-1

HINT
White could hit two men, run out to the 17-point or
make the 10-point. Which is right?

Solution to Puzzle 20

The right play is 23/13(2). This controls three-quarters of the board and gives the best chance of hitting the straggler on your bar-point. If your opponent hits on his two-point with a one or two, you can still win if you hit back.

TIP: EVEN A THREE-POINT BOARD GIVES YOU WINNING
CHANCES IF YOU CAN HIT A SHOT

23

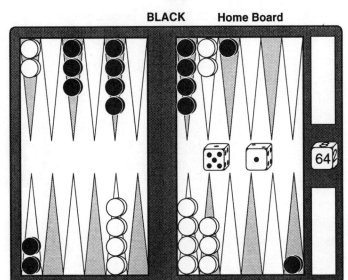

BLACK   **Home Board**

WHITE   **Home Board**

Money Game
White to play 5-1

HINT
White has to leave a shot with this awkward roll;
where is the best place to leave it?

Solution to Puzzle 21

Because Black has a blot in his board, the right play is to hit with
9/1*. This threatens a blitz attack and the win of a gammon, so
White can often "cash" the game next turn. The alternative 8/2 4/2
leaves only four shots, but Black can escape with any six.

Tip: It can often be right to hit on the ace-point
when you have a three-point board

24

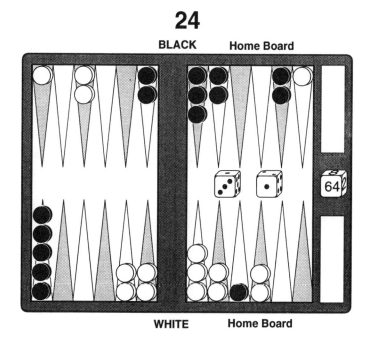

BLACK   Home Board

WHITE   Home Board

Money Game
White to play 3-1

HINT
Both sides have a three-point board here;
should White attack or play safe?

Solution to Puzzle 22

The right play by a small margin is 24/17. Although this leaves eight shots (6-1, 4-3, 5-3 and 6-3) White has secured a useful anchor and will be well-placed if not hit. 17/10 is a close second but hitting two men with 8/2*/1* is wrong because Black has the stronger board.

TIP: MAKING A FORWARD ANCHOR USUALLY JUSTIFIES
LEAVING SEVERAL SHOTS

25

BLACK   **Home Board**

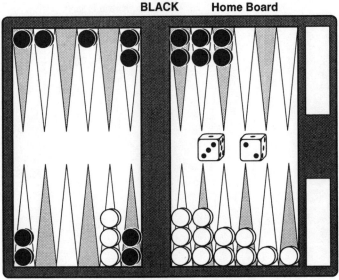

WHITE   **Home Board**

Double Match Point
White to play 3-2

HINT
All White has to do is to win the game;
what is the safest way to do this?

Solution to Puzzle 23

The right play here is to slot the bar with 8/7 and to hit on the ace-point with 6/1*. This maximises the chances of making the bar and the return hit should not be feared because Black has a weak board and White has a high anchor.

TIP: IF YOU SLOT THE BAR-POINT IT CAN BE RIGHT TO ALSO HIT ON THE ACE-POINT TO PROTECT THE BLOT

26

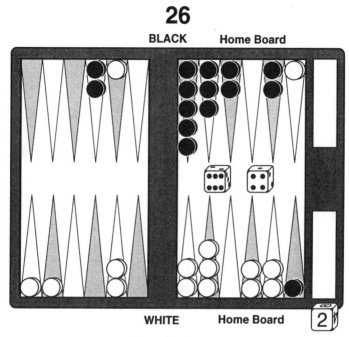

BLACK   Home Board

WHITE   Home Board

Money Game
White to play 6-4

Solution to Puzzle 24

The correct play is to hit with 7/4* but then to lift the blot with 4/3. Leaving the four-point slotted leaves extra shots and the reward does not justify the risk. The extra man on the three-point is still useful if Black enters on the ace- or deuce-point.

TIP: OFTEN IT IS BETTER NOT TO LEAVE A POINT SLOTTED
WHEN THERE ARE OTHER BLOTS AROUND THE BOARD

27

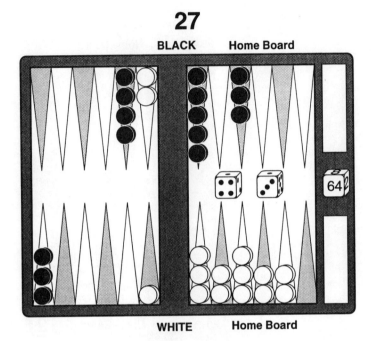

Money Game
White to play 4-3

HINT
White is a long way ahead in the race here.
What does that suggest?

Solution to Puzzle 25

The right move is 5/2 6/4, keeping three men on the eight-point.
White is so far ahead in the race that Black's best chance of winning
is to hit a shot. If White rolls 6-1 next time, White will not have to
give that shot, and White gets an extra roll to throw a winning double.

TIP: WHEN THE OPPONENT IS VERY UNLIKELY TO WIN TRY
TO AVOID GIVING HIM ANY CHANCES AT ALL

28

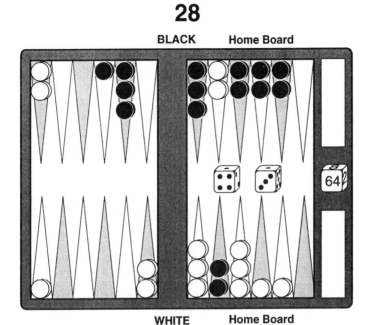

BLACK   Home Board

WHITE   Home Board

0-0 in a 5-point match
White to play 4-3

HINT
White can hit a blot and cover one of his own;
but is it the right play?

Solution to Puzzle 26

White should play 24/14. This escapes the back man and covers all the outfield if Black jumps out. True it leaves a direct ace, but if White stays on the 24-point Black will hit with fours or fives. Hitting on the ace-point with 5/1* still leaves White with work to do.

**TIP: TRY TO MINIMISE SHOTS WHEN YOUR OPPONENT HAS
A FOUR-POINT BOARD**

29

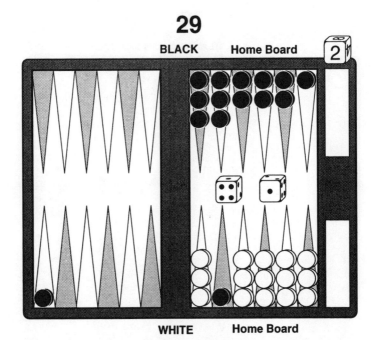

Money Game
White to play 4-1

HINT
**Black is unlikely to win if he doesn't hit a shot;
what is the best way to prevent that?**

Solution to Puzzle 27

White should make a dash for safety with 18/11. If Black misses,
White will double and Black will have to pass because he is so far
behind in the race. If Black hits he only has a two-point board at
present and White will be favourite to enter and escape.

**TIP: TRY TO LEAVE AN ANCHOR BEFORE YOUR
OPPONENT'S BOARD BECOMES TOO STRONG**

30

BLACK   Home Board

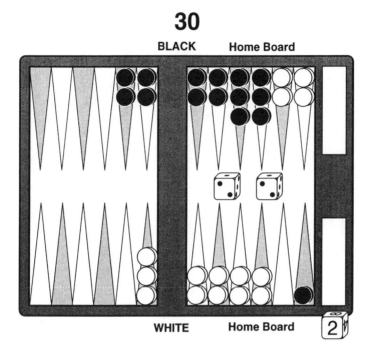

WHITE   Home Board   2

Money Game
White to play 2-2

HINT
White has four men stuck behind a prime; what is the
best way to keep some winning chances?

Solution to Puzzle 28

It is much too risky to hit here because White will have three loose
blots after doing so. Correct is 13/9 12/9, keeping the anchor and
restraining Black's back men. Only 6-2, 5-3 and 4-4 then hit for
Black and meanwhile his back men are becoming separated.

**TIP: DO NOT GIVE UP AN ANCHOR TO HIT WHEN YOU
LEAVE SHOTS AND THE OPPONENT HAS A STRONG BOARD**

31

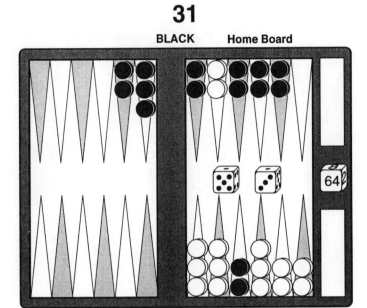

Money Game
White to play 5-3

HINT
**At some point White has to get his back men around;
is this the time to run?**

Solution to Puzzle 29

White should play 4/o 1/o. By taking two off he makes it much less likely that he will lose the race, and only 6/5 will leave a shot next turn. Hitting with 6/5* 5/1 does not take any men off and Black has a better chance of hitting a subsequent shot.

**Tip: Generally bear off if you can do so safely
when the opponent has one man back**

32

BLACK **Home Board**

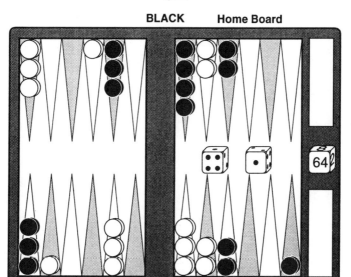

WHITE **Home Board**

Money Game
White to play 4-1

HINT
White can safety both blots here but is that best?

Solution to Puzzle 30

White should try to keep his timing by not hitting with 7/3 4/2(2). This stops Black escaping with a six and also means that Black will be forced to break his six-prime with a four or a five, unless it comes with a three.

TIP: IT IS USUALLY WRONG TO PUT YOUR OPPONENT ON
THE BAR WHEN HE HAS A SIX-PRIME

33

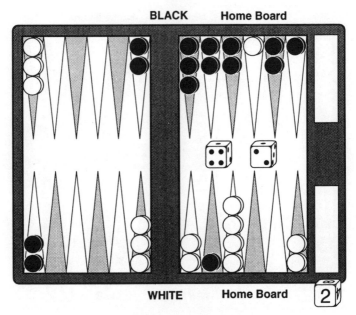

BLACK   Home Board

WHITE   Home Board

2

Money Game
White to play 4-2

Solution to Puzzle 31

White should leave the anchor now with 20/12. Although Black can then attack with twos and threes, White's strong board means that a return hit will win. If White waits, Black will come out himself and control the outfield.

TIP: YOU SHOULD BE PREPARED TO BREAK AN ANCHOR
WHEN YOU ARE RUNNING OUT OF TIMING

34

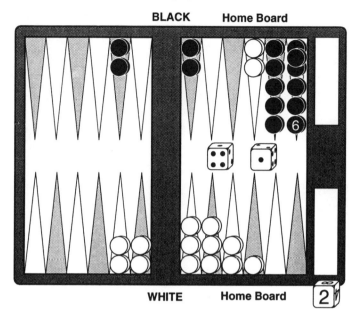

BLACK   Home Board

WHITE   Home Board

2-2 in an 11-point match
White to play 4-1

HINT
Black may well leave a shot next turn;
is it right to split the anchor here?

Solution to Puzzle 32
Even though it leaves a direct shot, White should make the bar-point with 11/7 8/7. Black only has a two-point board and White has an advanced anchor. The four-prime White makes is very strong, especially as Black has three checkers back.

TIP: MAKING A FOUR-PRIME IS USUALLY WORTH THE RISK

OF LEAVING A DIRECT SHOT

35

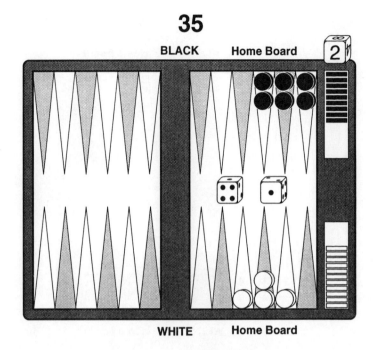

9-9 in an 11-point match
White to play 4-1

HINT
Black probably needs to roll a double here;
if he gets it White will need one himself

Solution to Puzzle 33

The right move is 7/5* 5/1 picking up the blot. It is too dangerous to leave the point slotted because of Black's strong board, but equally it is necessary to hit to take away half of Black's roll. White may be able to jump with a five or six next roll.

TIP: LOOK OUT FOR A "PICK AND PASS" PLAY IF YOUR
OPPONENT HAS A THREATENING POSITION

36

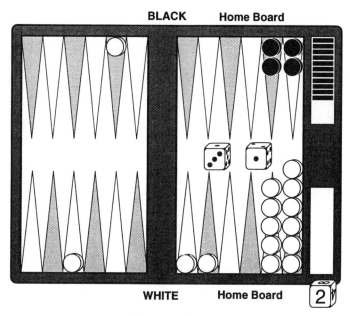

Money Game
White to play 3-1

HINT
**White is a big underdog to save the gammon here;
how do we give ourselves the best chance?**

Solution to Puzzle 34

The right play is to just to cover the blot with 8/3. This differs from Puzzle 5 in that to split the anchor here is a mistake because Black gains a lot on numbers such as 5-1 and 5-2 which he can use to "pick and pass". Most unpleasant of all for Black is 5-3.

TIP: COMPARE THE GAINS AND LOSSES WHEN SPLITTING AN
ANCHOR TO MAXIMISE SHOTS

37

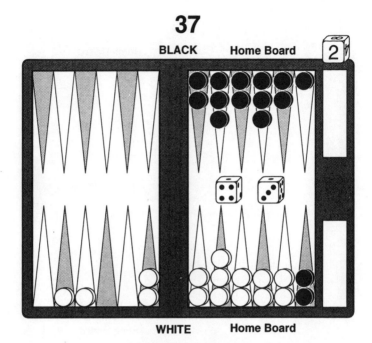

Money Game
White to play 4-3

Solution to Puzzle 35

If Black fails to get a double, White should win, so let us assume Black manages this. In that case the best move is 4/o 3/2 which ensures that 2-2 next turn will get all three men off. 4/o 2/1 is weaker because 2-2 next roll only removes two men.

TIP: IN THE BEAR-OFF CONSIDER WHICH DOUBLES WORK
AND WHETHER IT COSTS TO PLAY FOR THEM

38

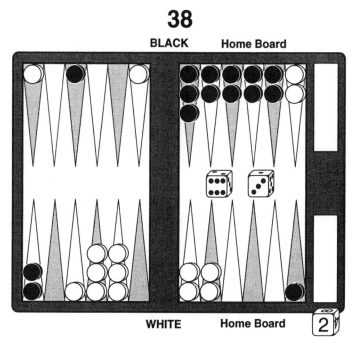

BLACK   Home Board

WHITE   Home Board

Money Game
White to play 6-3

Solution to Puzzle 36

The correct play is 17/14 5/4 which saves the gammon with a roll of
6-6, 5-5 or 4-4 next turn, assuming we do get another roll. Other
moves fail on either 5-5 or 4-4.

TIP: WHEN YOU ARE UNLIKELY TO SAVE THE GAMMON

TRY TO MAKE AS MANY DOUBLES WORK AS POSSIBLE

39

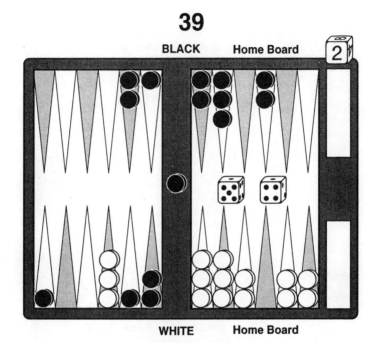

Money Game
White to play 5-4

HINT
Look at your opponent's good replies before considering your bad rolls next turn!

Solution to Puzzle 37

The correct play is to pile up the spare men on the bar-point with 11/7 10/7. This means that White cannot move a six next roll and that should hopefully slow him down while Black's board becomes weaker.

TIP: LOOK OUT FOR THE POSSIBILITY OF "KILLING" SIXES

WHEN BEARING IN AGAINST AN ACE-POINT ANCHOR

40

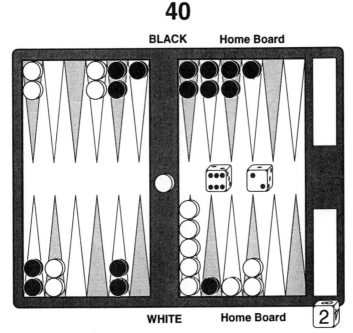

BLACK   **Home Board**

WHITE   **Home Board**

**Money game
White to play 6-2**

**HINT
The two is forced: b/23. Which of the
ugly sixes should White prefer?**

Solution to Puzzle 38

The correct play is to make the bar with 13/7 9/7. After this move
White is a slight underdog, whereas moves such as 18/15* 15/9
will allow Black to enter and later escape. Black needs a three to
hit and a three to get to the edge of White's prime – duplication.

**TIP: A FIVE-POINT PRIME PROVIDES TREMENDOUS
COMPENSATION FOR OTHER DEFECTS IN A POSITION**

41

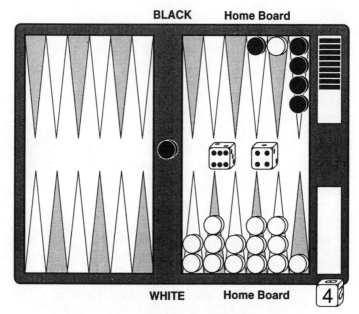

White trails 2-4 in an 11-point match
White to play 6-4

HINT
The six is forced: 23/17. Should White cover with the four or leave the man on the ace-point?

Solution to Puzzle 39

The correct play is 9/4 6/2. True this means that some of your sixes will leave a shot next turn, but the clever move 9/4 9/5 leaves your opponent an immediate six shots (6-3, 3-1 and 3-2) and the risk is not justified.

TIP: WHEN YOU ARE A BIG FAVOURITE, TRY TO AVOID
LEAVING ANY SHOTS AT ALL IF POSSIBLE

42

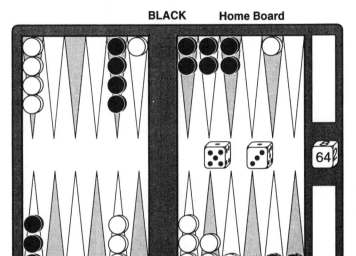

**Money Game
White to play 5-3**

Solution to Puzzle 40

All the sixes are unattractive, so White should hit by playing b/23
11/5*. Although this gives all fives and fours in reply, it takes away
half of Black's roll, which must be used to enter, and Black may roll
one of his four "dancing" numbers (6-6, 6-3 or 3-3).

**Tip: When you have to leave many shots anyway it
is usually best to hit**

43

BLACK   **Home Board**

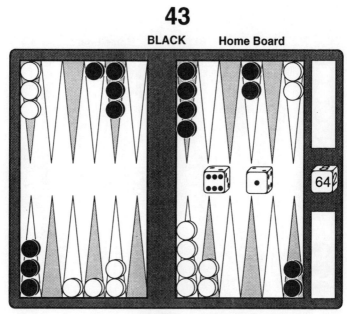

WHITE   **Home Board**

Money Game
White to play 6-1

HINT
**Making blocking points is usually a good idea, but
aggression must be combined with caution**

Solution to Puzzle 41

This is a continuation of the position in Puzzle 79 later in the book.
By a small margin it is right to cover on the ace-point with 23/17
5/1. White is about 50% to win the game then. If White plays 23/13
and Black hits, White is still an underdog to hit the second man.

**TIP: TRYING TO PICK UP A SECOND MAN IS RIGHT ONLY IF
YOU ARE A CLEAR UNDERDOG OTHERWISE**

44

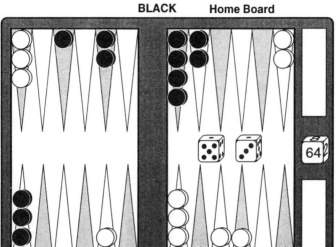

Money Game
White to play 5-3

HINT
White has a slightly better board;
how should he try to exploit this?

Solution to Puzzle 42

The right play is to make the opponent's bar with 23/18 and then to hit with 4/1*. Even if Black hits back White should soon enter and he has a fine defensive anchor. Pointing with 6/1* 4/1 still leaves White with the problem of extricating the two back men.

TIP: A PERMANENT ASSET SHOULD USUALLY BE
PREFERRED TO A SHORT-TERM GAIN

45

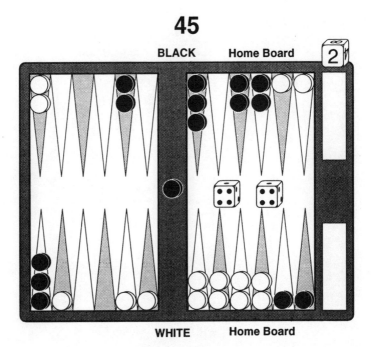

Money Game
White to play 4-4

HINT
White has a strong position here;
how does he take maximum benefit?

Solution to Puzzle 43

The right play is 24/18 10/9. This makes the useful nine-point and starts the escape of the back men. If Black hits, White will usually get return shots from the bar. Making the bar with 13/7 8/7 leaves too many indirect shots; 13/7 9/8 is bad if Black rolls a six.

TIP: COMING OUT TO THE OPPONENT'S BAR-POINT IS A GOOD PLAN IF HE ONLY HAS A TWO-POINT BOARD

46

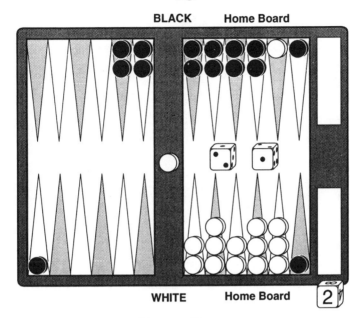

BLACK   **Home Board**

WHITE   **Home Board**

Money Game
White to play 2-1

> **HINT**
> **White is stuck behind a six-prime here;**
> **what is the best chance of causing it to break?**

Solution to Puzzle 44

In the opening it is usually right to hit on the five-point and therefore 8/5* is correct. White should use the five to hit on the ace-point with 6/1* and he will then have a strong double if Black does not hit back.

TIP: IF YOU HAVE A CHANCE TO HIT TWO MEN WHEN YOU HAVE A THREE-POINT BOARD IT IS USUALLY RIGHT

47

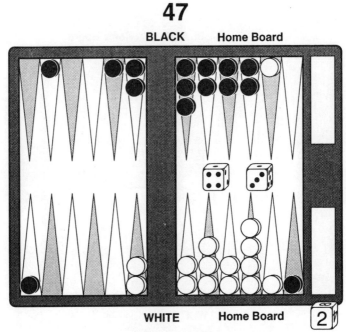

Money Game
White to play 4-3

HINT
**Black is threatening to make a six-prime with any five
or three; what should White do about this?**

Solution to Puzzle 45

White should be playing aggressively for the gammon with 6/2*(2)
5/1*(2), putting three men on the bar. The builders on the seven-,
eight- and 11-points can then be used to attack Black when he
enters. If Black anchors he is much less likely to be gammoned.

**TIP: LOOK FOR A "SWITCHING" PLAY TO STOP THE
OPPONENT ANCHORING WHEN YOU HAVE A STRONG BOARD**

48

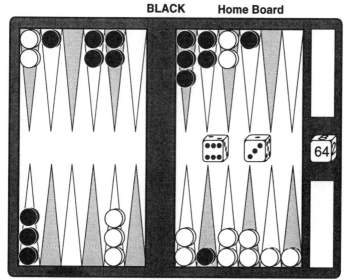

BLACK   Home Board

WHITE   Home Board

Money Game
White to play a 6-3

Solution to Puzzle 46

White should not hit, but should play b/23 5/4. This gives Black a couple of bad numbers (5/5 and 4/4) but more importantly it reduces the chances of being gammoned, which is a real danger here. If White hits he is likely to crash his board next roll.

TIP: SOMETIMES IT IS BETTER TO COME AN HONOURABLE
SECOND AND GIVE UP ON WINNING THE GAME

49

BLACK   Home Board

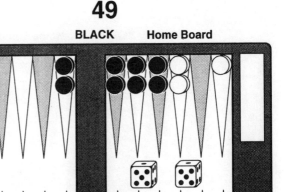

WHITE   Home Board

Money Game
White to play 5-5

HINT
**The main problem for White is the three men behind
Black's blockade. What does that suggest?**

Solution to Puzzle 47

White should play 5/1* 7/4. Although this leaves 20 shots and may
well lose a gammon, the risk is justified, because if Black does not
enter, White is well-placed to close Black out and escape his back
man, possibly winnning a gammon himself.

**TIP: ACT BEFORE THE OPPONENT MAKES A SIX-PRIME
AND NOT AFTERWARDS, EVEN IT INVOLVES A BIG RISK**

50

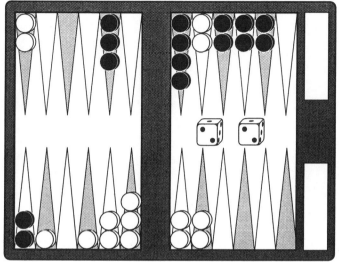

BLACK   Home Board

WHITE   Home Board

Double Match Point
White to play 2-2

> **HINT**
> Should White build his board or
> try to escape his back men?

Solution to Puzzle 48

The right play is the aggressive 8/2 8/5*. True, Black is slight favourite to hit back (20 numbers do so while 16 numbers stay on the bar) but Black is a bigger favourite if White does not hit. Moreover, White will be well-placed if Black stays on the bar.

TIP: WHEN YOU ARE AN UNDERDOG LOOK TO MAKE AN
AGGRESSIVE PLAY WHICH GAINS A LOT WHEN IT WORKS

Part Two:
Cube Decisions

51

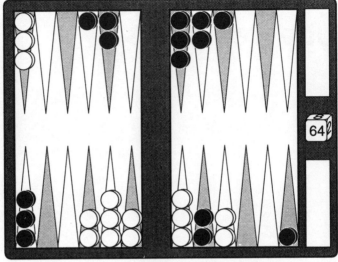

Money Game
Should White double?
Should Black take?

HINT
White has a number of safe landing points for his men
on the mid-point; what does this mean?

Solution to Puzzle 49

The right play is to bring the two men out with 22/17(2) and then to
point with 6/1*(2). This makes it harder for Black to safety the man
on his 16-point and provides a landing place for the man on the 24-
point which will move forward with any ace or deuce.

TIP: IT IS BETTER TO HAVE AN ANCHOR ON THE OUTSIDE
OF A PRIME THAN BEHIND IT

52

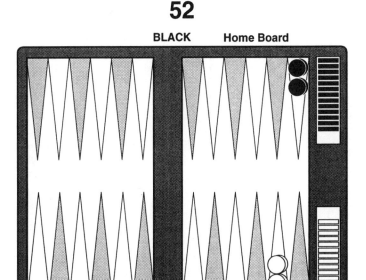

BLACK   Home Board

WHITE   Home Board   2

Money Game
Should White redouble?
Should Black take?

HINT
Count White's winning rolls

Solution to Puzzle 50

The right plan is to switch the anchor from the 20-point to the opponent's bar-point with 20/18(2) and then to play 11/9 7/5 keeping a five-prime. Black may later be forced to leave a double shot on his mid-point. You should have time to keep your mid-point here.

TIP: THE BEST DEFENSIVE ANCHOR IS THE BAR-POINT
WHEN THE OPPONENT STILL HAS TO CLEAR THE MID-POINT

53

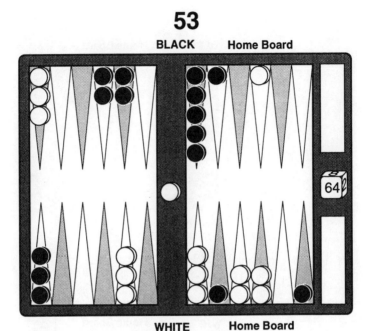

Money Game
Should White double?
Should Black take?

> **HINT**
> Think of the acronym PRAT – position, race and
> threats, as explained on page 10

Solution to Puzzle 51

This position is a double for White and Black should pass. White is much more likely to bring the position home safely when he has his bar-point, eight-point and nine-point already made. He can also attack the man on his one-point in some variations.

TIP: A HIGH ANCHOR IS LESS VALUABLE WHEN YOUR
OPPONENT HAS MADE SEVERAL POINTS IN FRONT OF IT

54

BLACK   Home Board

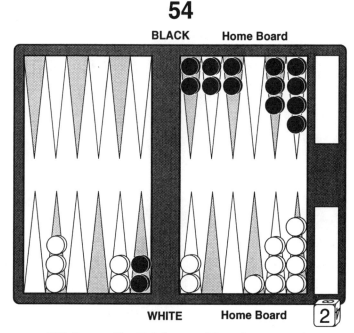

WHITE   Home Board |2|

White trails 7-8 in an 11-point match
Should White redouble?
Should Black take?

HINT
Think carefully before putting the match on the line;
sometimes it is better to live to fight another day

Solution to Puzzle 52

This is a standard position and is a redouble and take. White has 26 winning rolls and 10 losing rolls and therefore should double. Black should take, because, as we explained in the introduction, he is winning more than a quarter of the time.

TIP: IF YOUR OPPONENT HAS FEWER THAN 27 WINNING

NUMBERS YOU SHOULD ACCEPT THE CUBE

55

BLACK   Home Board

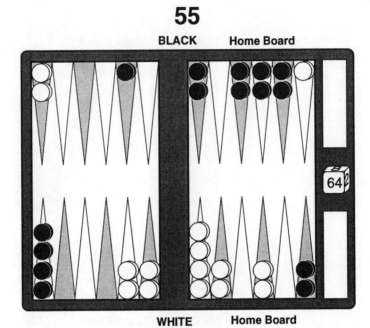

WHITE   Home Board

Money Game
Should White double?
Should Black take?

HINT
**White has the better blockade here but Black has a
four-point board**

Solution to Puzzle 53
The correct cube action in this position is for White to double and
for Black to accept. Although White has a three-point board, White
is on the bar and may not hit. The rolls of 6-1, 6-2, 6-3, 6-4 and 6-6 do
not hit, and if hit Black may make the golden anchor in reply.

**Tip: When your opponent is on the bar, you
should tend to accept a double**

56

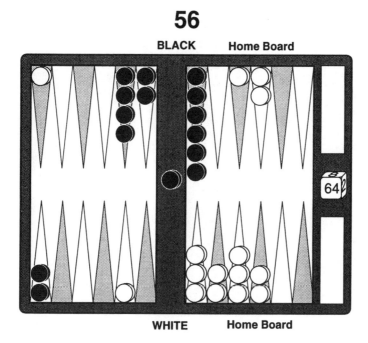

BLACK　　Home Board

WHITE　　Home Board

0-0 in an 11-point match
Should White double?
Should Black take?

HINT
Black is on the bar and has no board yet;
how significant are these factors?

Solution to Puzzle 54

The right decision is for White to redouble to four and for Black to pass. He will then trail 8-9, but that is better than playing this position for the match. White is ahead in the race and will get shots if Black has to leave next roll with a six.

Tɪᴘ: Tʜᴇ ʀᴀᴄᴇ ɪs ᴛʜᴇ ᴍᴏsᴛ ɪᴍᴘᴏʀᴛᴀɴᴛ ᴘᴀʀᴛ ᴏғ ᴛʜᴇ
ɢᴀᴍᴇ; ɪғ ʏᴏᴜ ᴀʀᴇ ʙᴇʜɪɴᴅ, ʏᴏᴜ ɴᴇᴇᴅ ᴄᴏᴍᴘᴇɴsᴀᴛɪᴏɴ

57

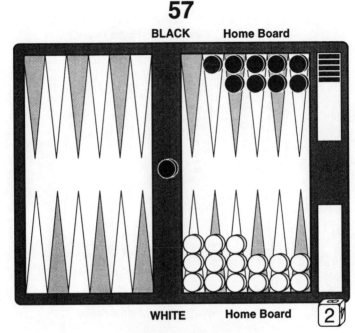

BLACK　　Home Board

WHITE　　Home Board

Money Game
Should White redouble?
Should Black take?

HINT
Black is going to be on the bar for a few rolls;
how likely is he to win when he gets in?

Solution to Puzzle 55

The correct action is for White to double and for Black to pass. White has several good numbers: 4/3 and 6/1 hitting, 6/5 escaping to the mid-point and a few numbers that make the four-point. A big drawback for Black is that he has no builders with which to attack.

TIP: ONE MAN BACK AGAINST TWO MEN BACK IS A DOUBLING ADVANTAGE. OTHER THREATS MAKE IT A PASS

58

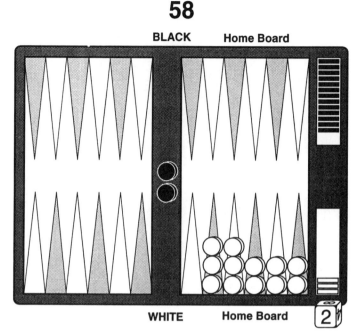

BLACK   Home Board

WHITE   Home Board

Money Game
Should White redouble?
Should Black take?

> **HINT**
> How likely is Black to get both men in and around
> before White bears off his remaining men?

Solution to Puzzle 56

White should double here and Black should pass. White has many numbers that make a five-point prime and if Black enters, White will readily attack because Black has no board. There should be plenty of time to escape the back three checkers later.

TIP: A MAN ON THE BAR AGAINST A FOUR-POINT BOARD
IS A PASS IF THE OPPONENT HAS BUILDERS IN POSITION

59

BLACK   **Home Board**

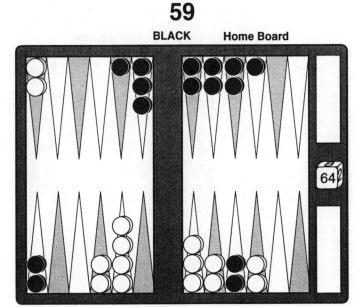

WHITE   **Home Board**

Money Game
Should White double?
Should Black take?

HINT
**Black has an anchor again and White is ahead
in the race; what is your decision?**

Solution to Puzzle 57

This position is a redouble for White and Black should pass. White
will probably take off two or three men before Black enters and
then Black still has to get round the board. In addition Black may
not bear off every time when he resumes bearing off.

T**IP:** A **MAN CLOSED OUT WITH FIVE MEN OFF IS A PASS**
UNLESS ALL YOUR OTHER NINE MEN ARE ON LOW POINTS

60

BLACK   Home Board

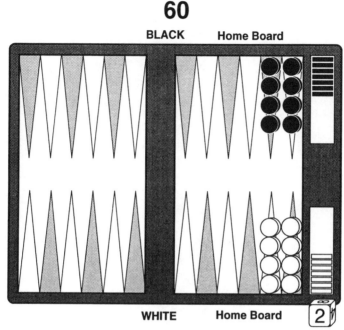

WHITE   Home Board   2

Money Game
Should White redouble?
Should Black take?

Solution to Puzzle 58

White should redouble and Black should accept. If Black does not get a six next roll, he will then have a pass, so White should double now. Black wins the game a little more than a quarter of the time and should therefore take.

**TIP: WITH TWO MEN ON THE BAR YOU NEED TO HAVE
BORNE OFF TEN MORE MEN THAN YOUR OPPONENT TO TAKE**

61

BLACK Home Board

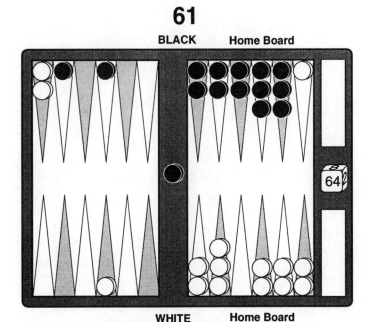

WHITE   Home Board

White trails 0-2 in a 7-point match
Should White double?
Should Black take?

HINT
**If you have a threat you should
consider a double**

Solution to Puzzle 59

White should double here and Black should accept. White has a
few rolls that improve his position and lose his market (most doubles
plus 5-4) but it could still be awkward clearing the mid-point. Black's
strong board means that he is likely to win if he hits a shot.

**TIP: TWO LANDING PLACES AGAINST THE FOUR-ANCHOR
IS A DOUBLE AND TAKE; THREE IS USUALLY A PASS**

62

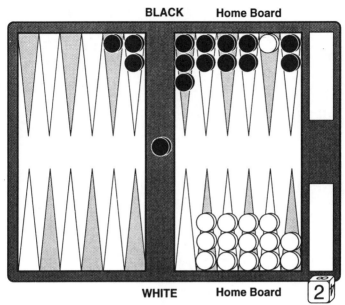

Money Game
Should White redouble?
Should Black take?

HINT
If the posiiton can change dramatically
next roll then consider a double

Solution to Puzzle 60
This position is a redouble and take with White winning almost 75% of the time. If neither side gets a double, White will win, but Black may be the only one to get a double. Black wins a fraction over a quarter of the time.

TIP: A FOUR-ROLL "NO MISS" POSITION IS AN INITIAL
DOUBLE OR A REDOUBLE AND A TAKE

63

BLACK   **Home Board**

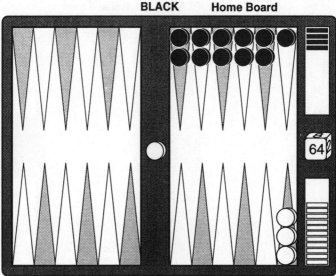

WHITE   **Home Board**

White leads 9-6 in an 11-point match
Should White double?
Should Black take?

> **HINT**
> If White hits with an ace he will be a big favourite but
> what happens if he misses, which is more likely?

Solution to Puzzle 61

The right decision is for White to double and for Black to accept.
Although White will probably win the game if he gets a six, and
may well win a gammon if he hits either or both of Black's loose
men, it may be several rolls before White gets his six.

**TIP: IF YOUR OPPONENT NEEDS A SIX TO GET OUT HE IS ONLY
ABOUT 30% TO GET IT EACH ROLL**

64

BLACK   Home Board

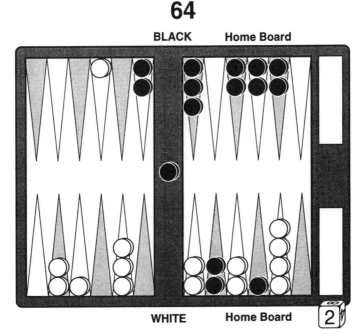

WHITE   Home Board

0-0 in an 11-point match
Should White redouble?
Should Black take?

HINT
Black has a man on the bar but it may be difficult for
White to bring his men home safely

Solution to Puzzle 62

The correct decision is for White to redouble and for Black to accept. If White rolls a six, he will almost certainly win and half his wins will be gammons, but Black may well get the six first, so he should accept.

TIP: IF THE FIRST SIX BY EITHER SIDE IS DECISIVE THEN
THE PLAYER ON ROLL IS ABOUT **70%** TO WIN

65

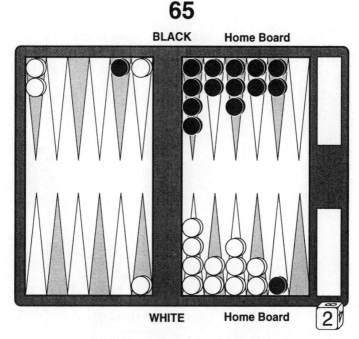

0-0 in an 11-point match
Should White redouble?
Should Black take?

> **HINT**
> All sixes and ones are good for White here and some
> numbers point on Black's blot

Solution to Puzzle 63

White should not double yet and Black has an easy take if doubled. Whilst any ace will make White a big favourite, he is only about 30% to get one, and Black will redouble to four immediately regardless. White may not enter for several rolls in this position.

TIP: ALWAYS ASSUME THAT YOU MISS A DIRECT SHOT AND EVALUATE THE RESULTING POSITION

66

BLACK   Home Board

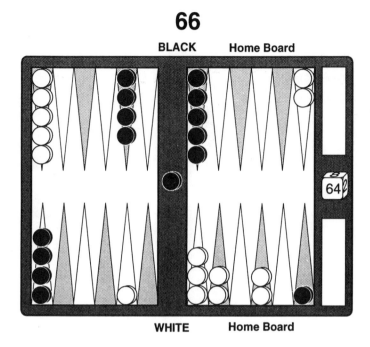

WHITE   Home Board

Money Game
Should White double?
Should Black take?

> **HINT**
> Black has done nothing to develop his position
> because White rolled well in the opening

Solution to Puzzle 64

White should not redouble yet and Black has an easy take. It is dangerous for White to attack on his three-point, and when Black enters he will have many chances of hitting a shot as White brings his men around.

TIP: THE FIVE-POINT ANCHOR AND A STRONG BOARD
COMBINE TO GIVE MANY CHANCES OF WINNING

67

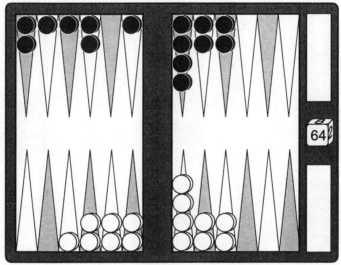

BLACK   Home Board

WHITE   Home Board

Money Game
Should White double?
Should Black take?

HINT
You need to count the race exactly and work out the
cube action from the advice on page 11

Solution to Puzzle 65

White should redouble here because so many numbers do
something effective. All aces hit, all sixes make the bar, and 5-4, 5-2,
4-2, 4-4 and 2-2 make the deuce point – a total of 28 good rolls.
Black can still take as he may jump out if White makes the bar.

TIP: YOU HAVE TO CONSIDER ALL YOUR OPPONENT'S
ROLLS NOT JUST THE STRONG ONES

68

BLACK   **Home Board**

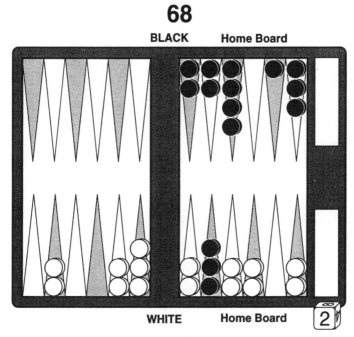

WHITE   **Home Board**

Money Game
Should White redouble?
Should Black take?

> **HINT**
> Black is 16 pips behind in the race;
> but White still has to get past the anchor

Solution to Puzzle 66

A common problem after an early 3-3 by White. This is a strong double but Black should still take despite his sorry development. White still has to do something about his back men and Black is likely to make an anchor at some stage.

TIP: BE WARY ABOUT GIVING UP THE GAME AFTER ONE STRONG ROLL BY THE OPPONENT

69

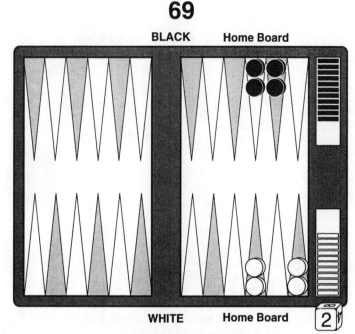

Money Game
Should White redouble?
Should Black take?

HINT
Here White will take two men off unless he rolls
a deuce; what does this mean?

Solution to Puzzle 67

The count in the race is 112-100 in White's favour, a lead of 12%.
This means that the position is a double and a bare take. If the
lead was just one pip more, then Black should pass; two pips fewer
and White should wait before doubling.

TIP: YOU NEED TO LEAD BY **MORE THAN 10%** IN A
LONG RACE TO DOUBLE; **UP TO 12%** IS A TAKE

70

BLACK Home Board

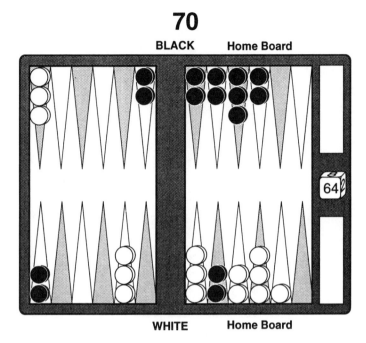

WHITE Home Board

Money Game
Should White double?
Should Black take?

HINT
White is ahead in the race but needs to bring his men
home safely; how likely is he to do this?

Solution to Puzzle 68

Although Black can win in two ways, by hitting a shot or by winning the race, White should redouble and Black should pass. Black's problem is that he needs a four or a five next turn to avoid having to waste pips in his home board.

TIP: THREE MEN ON AN ANCHOR IS WORSE THAN TWO IF
YOU MIGHT BE UNABLE TO MOVE ONE OF THEM NEXT ROLL

71

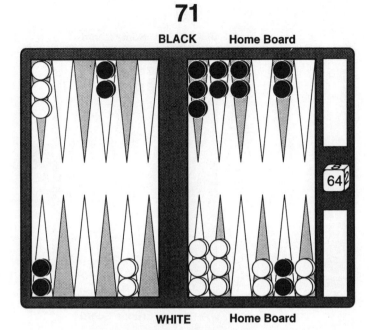

Money Game
Should White double?
Should Black take?

HINT
Black has a low anchor here; how does this affect the
assessment of the position?

Solution to Puzzle 69

This position is a redouble and Black should pass. If White does
not miss with a deuce, then Black needs a double and if White
does miss, Black can still miss with an ace himself.

**TIP: IF YOU HAVE FOUR MEN EACH AND YOU LEAD IN THE
PIP-COUNT IT IS USUALLY A DOUBLE AND A PASS**

72

BLACK   **Home Board**

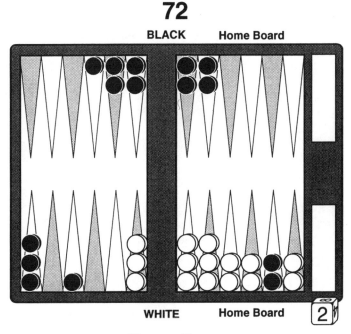

WHITE   **Home Board**

Money Game
Should White redouble?
Should Black take?

HINT
Here White is way ahead in the race and has a smooth
distribution; what should he do?

Solution to Puzzle 70

White has just enough of an advantage to double and Black should
take. Unless White rolls a double at some stage, he is very likely to
leave a shot, and Black may also get back into the race by rolling
a large double. Black, of course, still has to hit any shot he gets.

TIP: THE FIVE-POINT ANCHOR PROVIDES TREMENDOUS
COMPENSATION FOR A RACE DEFICIT IN A HOLDING GAME

73

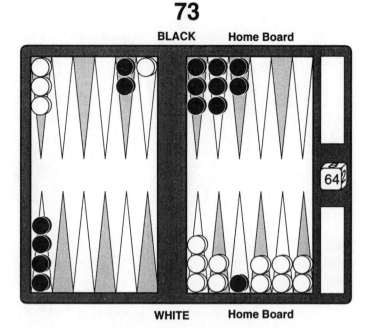

0-0 in an 11-point match
Should White double?
Should Black take?

HINT
**Both sides have a loose man; how significant
is White's stronger board?**

Solution to Puzzle 71

The correct decision is for White not to double and for Black to take. White still has a lot of work to do to bring the position home, and is forced to play his next six from the mid-point. Because of his two men on the ace-point it is harder for White to play safely.

**TIP: A LOW ANCHOR CAN BE MORE THAN ADEQUATE IF
THE OPPONENT HAS MEN OUT OF PLAY**

74

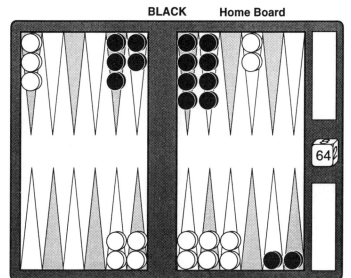

BLACK   Home Board

WHITE   Home Board

0-0 in an 11-point match
Should White double?
Should Black take?

HINT
White has the better prime here;
how significant is that?

Solution to Puzzle 72

This position is so strong for White that he is too good to redouble and should play on hoping to get a gammon. Sometimes he will leave a shot, but Black still has to hit it and White always has the option to double later.

> **TIP: YOU CAN PLAY ON AGAINST A LOW ANCHOR WHEN**
> **YOU ARE VERY LIKELY TO WIN A GAMMON IF NOT HIT**

75

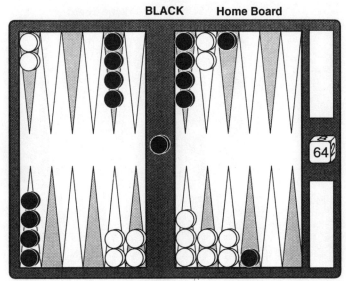

BLACK   Home Board

WHITE   Home Board

0-0 in an 11-point match
Should White double?
Should Black take?

HINT
White has a five-prime and Black is on the bar;
how big is this advantage?

Solution to Puzzle 73

White should double here and Black should pass. If White rolls a
two or a nine, he will hit on his four-point and Black is in danger of
getting gammoned if he does not hit back. Also, if Black does safety
his blot, White is a big favourite to win the race.

TIP: EVEN A SMALL DANGER OF A GAMMON MAY CAUSE
YOU TO PASS WHEN YOU ARE AN UNDERDOG

76

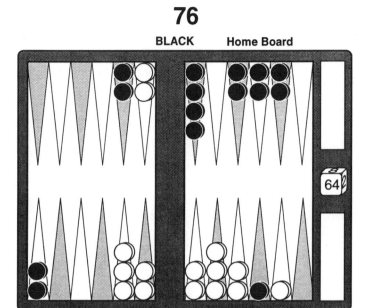

BLACK   Home Board

WHITE   Home Board

White leads 8-7 in an 11-point match
Should White double?
Should Black take?

HINT
Before doubling consider how strong
your threats really are

Solution to Puzzle 74

White has a very strong position and should double and Black should pass. White has plenty of time to jump out with the back men and nearly all Black's high numbers have to be played by burying men in his board.

> **TIP: A FIVE-PRIME WITH MEN BEHIND IT COMBINED WITH A**
> **GOOD ANCHOR IS USUALLY A DOUBLE AND A PASS**

77

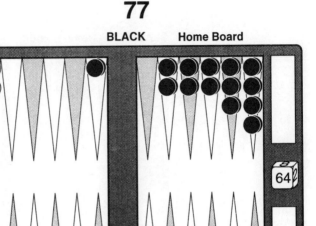

BLACK   Home Board

WHITE   Home Board

0-0 in a 5-point match
Should White double?
Should Black take?

HINT
White is favourite to hit here;
but what happens if he misses?

Solution to Puzzle 75

White has a very strong position here with a high anchor and a five-prime and instead of doubling should play on for a gammon. If doubled Black should pass. If Black makes an anchor White may then reconsider doubling, but at the moment he should play on.

TIP: WHEN YOU HAVE A BIG ADVANTAGE CONSIDER
PLAYING FOR AN UNDOUBLED GAMMON

78

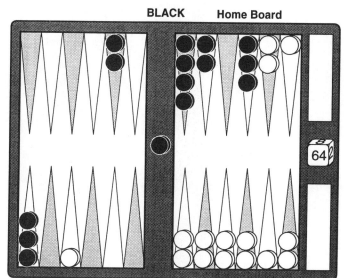

White trails 6-9 in an 11-point match
Should White double?
Should Black take?

> **HINT**
> **If White covers the man on the two-point he should**
> **have time to escape and win**

Solution to Puzzle 76

The correct decision is for White not to double yet. There are a few crushing rolls such as 5-5 and 5-2, but Black leads in the race and White will be wary of hitting loose because of Black's strong board. Black may later redouble for the match as he only needs four points.

TIP: WHEN YOUR OPPONENT IS AT THE EDGE OF YOUR PRIME DO NOT DOUBLE BEFORE POINTING ON HIM

79

BLACK   **Home Board**

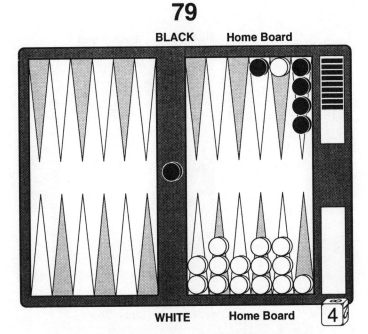

WHITE   **Home Board**

White trails 2-4 in an 11-point match
Should White redouble?
Should Black take?

HINT
**If you close out two men you are always a favourite
especially if the opponent has other men on the board**

Solution to Puzzle 77

The correct decision is not to double yet. Black should obviously accept if doubled. Although 24 numbers hit on White's bar-point, Black will have a return shot on most of them. The 12 numbers that miss usually mean that Black will redouble.

TIP: IF YOU MAKE A DOUBLE BASED ON A THREAT, THEN
BE SURE THAT THE THREAT IS DECISIVE

80

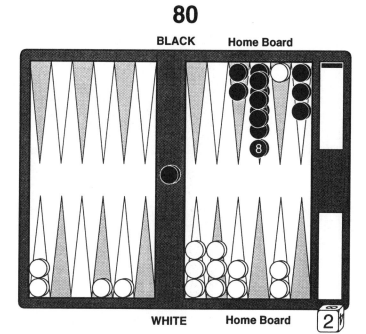

BLACK Home Board

WHITE Home Board

White leads 3-2 in an 11-point match
Should White redouble?
Should Black take?

HINT
Black has an ugly position with his crushed board but
there are no marks for beauty in backgammon

Solution to Puzzle 78

This is a correct, but only marginal double and easy take for Black.
If White covers this turn, which is unlikely anyway, many rolls then
cause White's board to crash next turn. Otherwise, Black can win
by throwing a deuce before White covers.

TIP: A FIVE-POINT BOARD AGAINST A MAN ON THE BAR IS
A DOUBLE BUT A TAKE IF THE BOARD MAY CRASH LATER

81

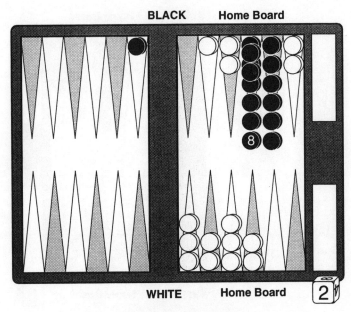

Money Game
Should White redouble?
Should Black take?

HINT
All sixes, threes and twos hit here.
But what happens if you miss?

Solution to Puzzle 79

There are many things that can go wrong for White here and it is premature to redouble. If White hits with an ace, then he will have a strong double, whether or not Black replies with an ace. However if White misses, Black is about equal – and White is favourite to miss.

TIP: LOOK AT THE BAD ROLLS RATHER THAN THE GOOD
ONES IN EVALUATING A POSITION

82

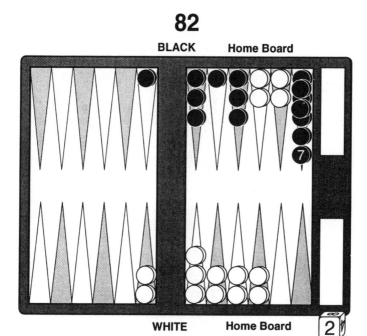

Money Game
Should White redouble?
Should Black take?

> **HINT**
> White is hitting with all twos, threes, fours and fives;
> what conclusion do you draw?

Solution to Puzzle 80

White should redouble here and Black should take. All White's pieces are well-placed for making new points and containing the Black checker when it enters. However, Black scrambles round often enough to take the cube.

TIP: A FOUR-POINT BOARD WITH THE OPPONENT ON THE
BAR IS A STRONG DOUBLE AND A MARGINAL TAKE

83

BLACK   Home Board

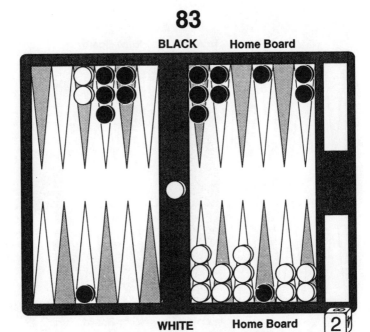

WHITE   Home Board   2

0-0 in a 5-point match
Should White redouble?
Should Black take?

HINT
White has a five-point board and is shooting at a blot;
what happens if he doesn't hit it?

Solution to Puzzle 81

This is a common position when you get a multiple shot from a backgame. It is too early to redouble. Although you are a big favourite to hit (only 5-5, 4-4, 5-4 and 4-1 miss) Black can still scramble round after you do. If you miss, however, you are likely to get gammoned.

**TIP: EVEN IF YOU GET A TRIPLE SHOT FROM A
BACKGAME, WAIT TO HIT IT FIRST**

84

BLACK   **Home Board**

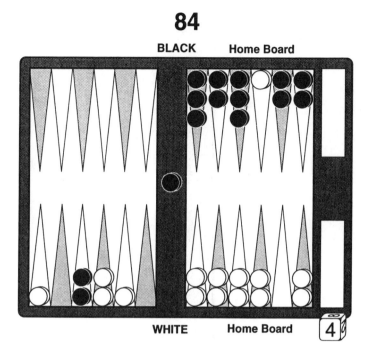

WHITE   **Home Board**   ⌊4⌋

0-0 in a 5-point match
Should White redouble?
Should Black take?

HINT
**Black is on the bar against a five-point board;
should White put the match on the line?**

Solution to Puzzle 82

White's threats are strong enough here to double, although it is quite rare to have a correct redouble before hitting in a back game, and Black should pass because he can still be gammoned if both men are picked up. White is very likely to contain any hit checkers.

> TIP: A QUADRUPLE SHOT WHICH IS LIKELY TO WIN IS A
> DOUBLE AND USUALLY A PASS

85

BLACK   **Home Board**

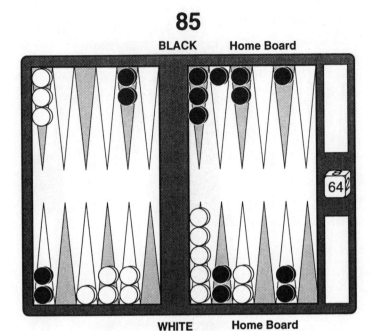

WHITE   **Home Board**

Money Game
Should White double?
Should Black take?

HINT
Black has two anchors here but White is way ahead in
the race; how do you assess these factors?

Solution to Puzzle 83

This is a strong redouble for White but a correct take. White hits
with all threes, 5-2, 5-4, 4-4, 2-2, 2-1 and 4-1, a total of 21 rolls, but
that means 15 numbers miss. If Black is hit, he may roll a three in
response and retain winning chances. Nine numbers don't enter.

TIP: IF YOUR OPPONENT IS ON THE BAR AGAINST A THREE-
POINT BOARD THAT MAY BE ENOUGH TO TAKE

86

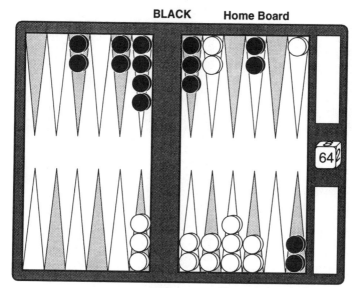

BLACK   Home Board

WHITE   Home Board

0-0 in a 5-point match
Should White double?
Should Black take?

> **HINT**
> White has all the advantages here with the anchor
> and the five-prime trapping Black's back men

Solution to Puzzle 84

White has a correct redouble and Black should take. The point is that if Black gives up he will be 4-0 down, so he should accept the not inconsiderable winning chances from this position. He needs to get a two quickly but his strong board then gives him chances.

TIP: YOU CAN TAKE QUITE UNFAVOURABLE POSITIONS IF OTHERWISE YOUR OPPONENT WOULD HAVE A BIG LEAD

87

BLACK   **Home Board**

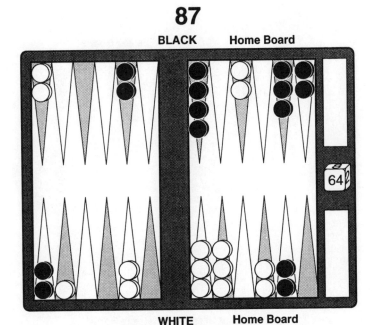

WHITE   **Home Board**

0-0 in a 5-point match
Should White double?
Should Black take?

HINT
**White has a more advanced anchor and Black has a
man wasted on his two-point**

Solution to Puzzle 85

It is too early for White to double and Black should obviously accept
if doubled. Black can either keep both anchors or can run from the
23-point, and White stil! has a lot of work to bring his men in safely.
Although Black has two blots in his board they will soon be covered.

**TIP: MOST POSITIONS WITH TWO ANCHORS ARE AN EASY
TAKE UNTIL A PRIME IS BUILT IN FRONT OF THEM**

88

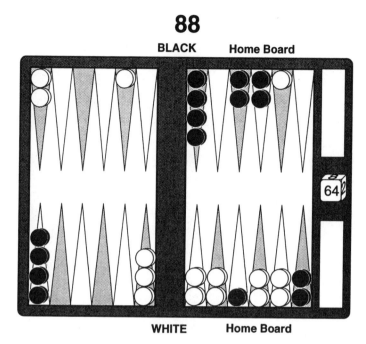

BLACK   Home Board

WHITE   Home Board

White leads 2-1 in a 5-point match
Should White double?
Should Black take?

Solution to Puzzle 86

White's advantages are in fact so great that White should play on and try for a gammon. The "sentry" on the 24-point makes it awkward for Black to play his moves safely but White must double later if things get sticky. Were White to double, Black should pass like a shot.

Tip: When you have a large advantage which is unlikely to dissipate, play for the gammon

89

BLACK   **Home Board**

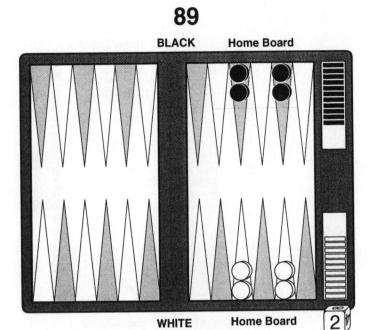

WHITE   **Home Board**

Money Game
Should White redouble?
Should Black take?

HINT
Either side may get off in one roll or two rolls;
but White is rolling first

Solution to Puzzle 87
The correct action is for White to double and for Black to take. Although Black has problems playing his next six, White has to move first and Black has race chances and no blots. At some point White will have to leave Black's four-point and then Black can attack.

TIP: THE BETTER ANCHOR CAN BE ENOUGH TO DOUBLE

BUT IT IS USUALLY A TAKE

90

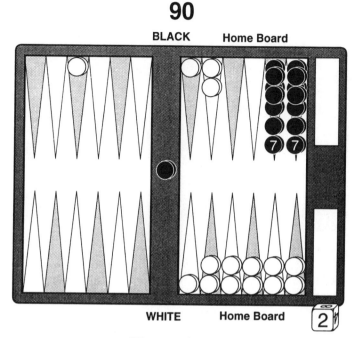

BLACK   Home Board

WHITE   Home Board

Money Game
Should White redouble?
Should Black take?

HINT
If White closes out Black he will almost certainly win;
how likely is that to happen?

Solution to Puzzle 88

Although White can still win a gammon here, it is better to double
and Black should pass. If Black makes an anchor on his 21-point
his position will improve dramatically, so White should double now
before that happens. Black is very close to a take already.

TIP: A BIRD IN THE HAND IS WORTH TWO IN THE BUSH;
ONLY PLAY FOR A GAMMON WHEN THE RISK IS SMALL

91

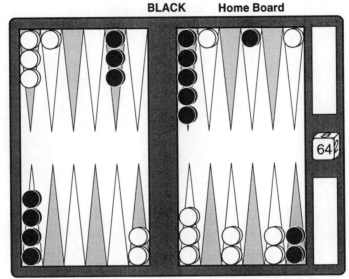

BLACK   Home Board

WHITE   Home Board

Money Game
Should White double?
Should Black take?

HINT
White's development is much better and
he has a direct shot

Solution to Puzzle 89

This position is a correct redouble and a correct take. White may "miss" with an ace or a three, but so may Black. The point is that even if White misses, Black cannot redouble, so White should redouble now as 4-4, 5-5 and 6-6 all win immediately.

TIP: FOUR MEN EACH IN A SYMMETRICAL POSITION IS A
DOUBLE; IF THE DOUBLER IS LIKELY TO MISS IT IS A TAKE

92

BLACK   Home Board

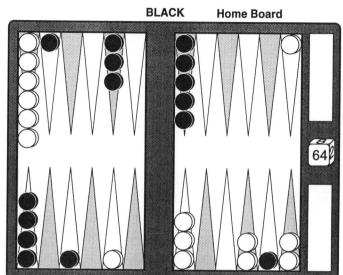

WHITE   Home Board

Money Game
Should White double?
Should Black take?

HINT
White has the better board but
Black has no man on the bar

Solution to Puzzle 90

White should redouble here and Black should accept. Despite Black's crushed board, he can still win by getting a six before White covers. Only 3-3, 6-3 and 5-4 cover, and Black will otherwise have a chance to hit the blot on White's six-point.

TIP: IF YOU ARE NOT CERTAIN TO BE CLOSED OUT AND
LEAD IN THE RACE, YOU CAN OFTEN SCRAMBLE HOME

93

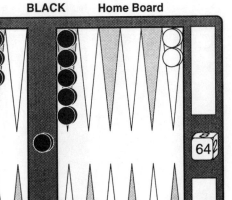

BLACK   Home Board

WHITE   Home Board

Money Game
Should White double?
Should Black take?

HINT
Here White has sixes and ones to hit a second
checker; are the threats strong enough?

Solution to Puzzle 91

White should double and despite his ugly position Black should accept. Black has an anchor and White has not yet made his five-point and is not favourite to hit with a deuce. Any further deterioration in Black's position would make it a pass.

TIP: BE MORE INCLINED TO TAKE WHEN YOU HAVE AN
ANCHOR AND THE OPPONENT HAS NOT MADE HIS FIVE-POINT

94

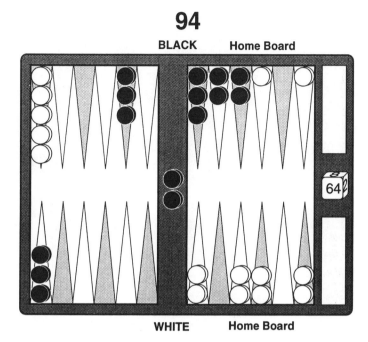

Money Game
Should White double?
Should Black take?

HINT
Black has two men on the bar against a four-point board; how serious is this?

Solution to Puzzle 92

It is a mistake for White to double here and Black should accept. Although White has a three-point board, he is unlikely to carry out a successful attack on Black's two loose blots.

TIP: IF YOUR OPPONENT IS NOT ON THE BAR, YOU
USUALLY NEED A FOUR-POINT BOARD TO DOUBLE IN A
BLITZ POSITION

95

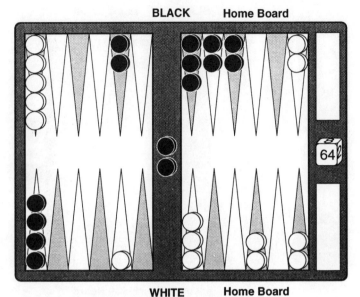

Money Game
Should White double?
Should Black take?

HINT
Black has been caught with two men on the bar;
how strong are White's threats?

Solution to Puzzle 93
White should double and Black has the barest of takes. This is a
blitz position and White will attack as vigorously as he can. Although
Black gets gammoned over half the time when he loses, he also
wins just enough games to eke out a take.

TIP: ONE MAN ON THE BAR AGAINST A THREE-POINT BOARD IS
NORMALLY A DOUBLE AND TAKE

96

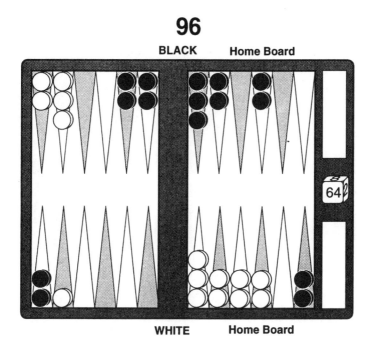

BLACK   **Home Board**

WHITE   **Home Board**

White leads 9-6 in an 11 point match
Should White double?
Should Black take?

HINT
For money, an ace-point game is a double and pass;
does the match score change the situation here?

Solution to Puzzle 94

Black has a lot of compensation here with three points in his home board and it is premature for White to double. It will be a while before White makes any more inner-board points and Black should, of course, accept a double.

TIP: LOOK AT THE STRENGTHS OF BOTH BOARDS *AND*

THE CHANCES THAT THEY WILL GET STRONGER

97

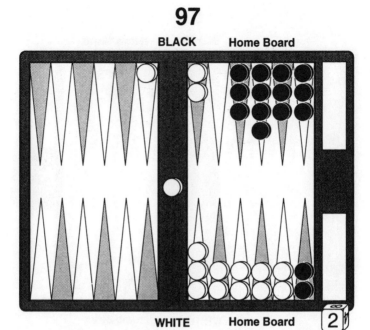

BLACK   Home Board

WHITE   Home Board

White leads 5-1 in an 11-point match
Should White redouble?
Should Black take?

HINT
It seems as if White will enter before Black can
escape his back men but he is not certain to do so

Solution to Puzzle 95

Even though White may make a fourth point, Black's strong board
means that he has an easy take, and it is premature for White to
double. Black is about even money in this position and is quite
close to a beaver.

**TIP: BEWARE OF DOUBLING A BLITZ WHEN YOU HAVE
WORK TO DO ON BOTH SIDES OF THE BOARD**

98

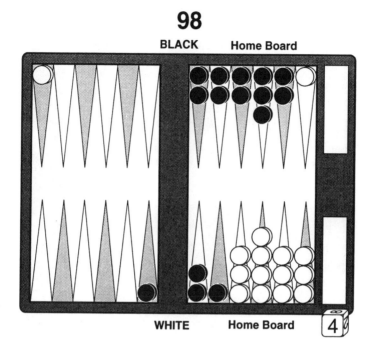

BLACK **Home Board**

WHITE **Home Board**

White trails 1-5 in an 11-point match
Should White redouble?
Should Black take?

Solution to Puzzle 96

At this score, White should not double yet and Black has an easy
take with an automatic redouble next turn, of course. The point is
that winning four points from a gammon is of no extra benefit to White.
In addition there is still work to do clearing the 13- and 14-points.

**TIP: WHEN YOU ARE TWO POINTS AWAY THINK OF
CONTINUING IF YOU CAN STILL WIN A GAMMON**

99

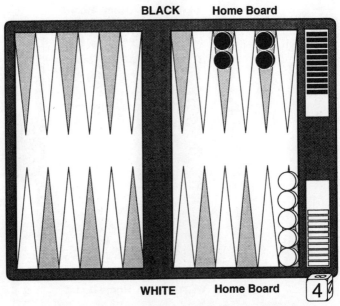

White trails 7-15 in a 25-point match
Should White redouble?
Should Black take?

HINT
White has five men against six here;
how likely is Black to miss?

Solution to Puzzle 97

Surprisingly White should hold on to the cube. If Black is forced to run with a six White has a good chance of a gammon, but Black should still accept as he is ahead in the race and can redouble to eight if things go well. Black can even win the match in this game!

TIP: BEWARE OF HIGH CUBES WHEN YOU ARE LEADING IN
THE MATCH UNLESS THE POSITION IS VERY SIMPLE

100

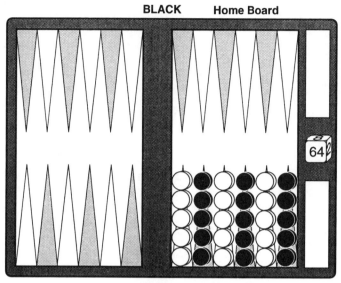

Money Game
Should White double?
Should Black take?

> **HINT**
> A very unusual position to conclude the book. How
> likely is Black to hit a shot?

Solution to Puzzle 98

A continuation of the last position, with colours reversed. White should redouble to eight, even though he is the underdog in this position. If he hits with a six and Black does not enter there are chances of winning a gammon for the match. Black has an easy take.

TIP: LOOK FOR A HIGH CUBE WHEN YOU ARE THE
TRAILER *BEFORE* YOU EXECUTE ANY THREATS

Solution to Puzzle 99

White should redouble to eight here and Black should accept. White will be a long way behind (7-19) if he loses, so he should take this chance to get back into the match. Black is likely to miss with an ace or a three over the next two rolls, but he may not, so he should take.

> TIP: IF YOUR OPPONENT HAS TWO GAPS HE IS SLIGHT
> FAVOURITE TO MISS ON EACH ROLL

Solution to Puzzle 100

White should not double yet as he is almost 95% to leave shots in the bear-off and Black will build a rolling prime, called a snake, which will slowly but inexorably consume its victim. The position is almost a "beaver" for money, but as Black gets gammoned and backgammoned a fair amount, he should just take.

> TIP: BEWARE OF BACK GAMES WHERE THE OPPONENT
> HAS THREE POINTS IN YOUR BOARD AND PERFECT TIMING

Computer Programs

The two strongest computer programs are Snowie and Jellyfish. The former, at the time of writing, is available as version 2.0, the latter as version 3.5. All positions in this book have been tested on both Snowie and Jellyfish, who agreed with the author with the exception of position 100 which is beyond their comprehension. Indeed Snowie beavers the redouble after being hit in the bear-off!

Jellyfish is available in three versions: Player (£24/$30), Tutor (£63/$100) and Analyser (£136/$220) and naturally the functions offered increase as the price rises. The web site http://jelly.effect.no/ allows you to download a trial freeware version.

Snowie has four versions: Professional ($350), Champion ($220), Student ($100) and Player ($39). For sterling prices contact BIBA (see page 127). Full details are available on the Internet at www.backgammon.thex.it/e-snowie.html or by telephone to (39) 347 4529409 or fax to (39) 045 7420449 or by email to snowie@thex.it

Both are available from the suppliers listed on page 127.

Glossary

This glossary contains all the terms the player will meet in this book together with many of the colourful expressions the player will meet if playing backgammon socially or in tournaments

Ace   A roll of one on a die. The ace-point is the one point

Anchor   A point in the opponent's home board, occupied by two or more of your checkers

Automatic Double   By agreement in a money game only, if both players roll the same number on the initial roll, the cube is automatically placed on two, but remains centered

Backgame   A position in which you have two or more anchors in the opponent's board and aim to hit a shot as he attempts to bring his checkers into his board

Backgammon The win of three times the value of the cube when the opponent still has one or more men in your home board or on the bar and has not borne off a checker

Baffle Box   A device, sometimes used, into which dice are thrown when rolling. It contains a helter-skelter of three slopes which ensures that the roll is fair

Bar   The central dividing area between the two halves of the board on which hit checkers are placed

Bar-point   A player's seven-point

Bear Off   To take a checker off the board in the closing stages; the stage when one or both players has all their men in the home board

Beaver   To double the value of an offered cube while retaining ownership of the cube on your side of the board

Blot   A single vulnerable man of either colour occupying a point

Blitz   An attack on one or more of your opponent's back men with the aim of repeatedly sending them to the bar

Blockade   Any series of points, whether consecutive or not, which prevents the opponent playing particular numbers

Board   The points made in a player's home board, e.g. a four-point board

Box   In a chouette, the player who is on his own

Boxes   A roll of double sixes

Broken Prime   A prime with a gap in it

Builder   A spare man, usually on one of the points from a player's 11-point to his seven-point, which can be used to make a point in board on a future roll

Captain   In a chouette, the member of the team who takes the final decision on checker plays

Centered Cube   One that has not yet been turned in that game, and shows 64, although its real value is one

Checker   One of the 30 round pieces used for playing the game

Chouette   A form of money game in which one player (the box) plays against other players (the team) one of whom (the captain) is rolling and making the checker plays. Each player has his own cube and makes his own decisions whether to take or pass

Close(d) Out   When one or more checkers are on the bar against a six-point home board

Cocked Die   A die which has not come to rest flat in the player's right-hand side of the board or which is on top of a checker

Contact   A situation where the possibility of hitting a shot still exists

Count   To add up the number of pips required to bear off all the remaining checkers. The count is the total so reached for both sides

Crash   To be forced to break the six-point and possibly other points in your home board; also called to crunch

Crawford Rule   In tournament matches only, the rule by which, in the game immediately after one player reaches a score one point from victory, the cube may not be used

Cross-over   A move from one quarter of the board to another

Cube   The doubling cube which starts in the centre of the board and may be used by either player to increase the value of the game

Dance   To fail to enter from the bar

Desmonds   Slang for the roll of double twos. Apparently named after Desmond Tutu

Deuce   A roll of two on a die; the two-point is also known as the deuce-point

Direct Shot   Any situation where a blot is six or less pips away from an opponent's checker

Diversification   Placing one's checkers such that the maximum number of rolls will play well on the next throw

Double   Any roll of the same number on each die. Any offer of a cube or to offer the cube

Double Shot   A blot exposed to two different direct shots

Drop   To reject or pass an offered cube

Duplication   A situation where one or more of the opponent's rolls offers a choice between different hitting or point-making moves thus reducing the number of good rolls which the opponent may throw

Enter   To roll a number corresponding to a point not occupied by two or more of your opponent's checkers and to move the man on the bar to that point

Equity   The average expected amount that will be won or lost in that particular game. For example, if you are certain to win a backgammon, your equity is +3

Fan   American slang for failing to enter from the bar

Flunk   More American slang for failing to enter from the bar

Gammon   The win of twice the value of the cube when the opponent has not borne off any checkers, but he has no men in your home board or on the bar

Golden Anchor   The opponent's five-point; your 20-point

Golden Point   Your five-point

Hit   To move a checker to a point occupied by only one of your opponent's checkers, thereby sending it to the bar

Hit Loose   To hit a blot in your home board thereby giving your opponent an opportunity to hit the same man from the bar

Holding Game   A situation in which a player has an anchor and is waiting to get a shot or to run with a double

Home Board   The six points from one to six from which the player bears off

Indirect shot   Any situation where a blot is seven or more pips away from an opponent's checker and there is a roll of the dice which will allow the opponent to hit it

Inner Board   The home board

Jacoby Paradox   A position in the bear-off, with one man on each of the five- and two-points, which strangely is not a redouble if the opponent will offer you a takeable cube when you miss, but is if he will cash the game when you miss

Jacoby Rule   The rule, usually employed in money games, that a gammon or backgammon does not count until an initial double has been made

Kauder Paradox   A rare position which is a correct double and a correct beaver. It can only apply in a money game

Latto Paradox   A very rare position, only in a money game, which is a correct redouble but not an initial double

Lipped Cups   Cups that have a ridge at the top to prevent the dice being rolled in an unfair way by a dice mechanic

Lover's Leap   An opening roll of 6-5 played by moving a checker from the 24-point to the mid-point

Man A term commonly used for a checker

Mechanic Someone who can cheat by rolling the dice in such a way that certain numbers appear with a greater frequency than they should. Also known as a dice mechanic

Mid-point The player's 13-point

Miss To fail to hit a shot, or, in the bear-off, to roll a number which has to be moved without taking off a checker

No Dice Slang for a faulty roll or for cocked dice

Outer Board The area of the board from one player's 13-point to his seven-point

Outside Prime A sequence of four or more points, none of which is in the player's home board

Pass To reject an offered cube

Pick and Pass To hit a blot with one part of the roll and to continue with the same checker to an occupied point

Pigeon Slang for a weak player who is prepared to play for money against stronger players

Point Any of the 24 triangles on which the checkers are placed; more commonly, such a triangle occupied by two or more of a player's checkers. To point on a checker is to move two men to the point occupied by an opponent's checker

Precision Dice Dice manufactured with extreme accuracy which should produce numbers with the correct frequency

Premature Roll A roll made before the opponent has completed his play by picking up his dice

Prime A sequence of at least four consecutive points each occupied by two or more men of the same colour

Raccoon After an initial double has been beavered, to turn the cube to double its previous value, while allowing the opponent to retain it on his side of the board

Race A position where all, or virtually all, contact has been broken and the possibility of hitting shots is minimal

Redouble Any double made subsequent to the initial double

Return A shot from the bar against one of the opponent's checkers immediately after being hit

Roll-out A means of evaluating the equity of a position by playing a large number of games from that position

Run To move a back man into the outer board

Settlement An agreement to end the game with a certain number of points being paid by one player to others

Shake To mix the dice using the dice cups prior to rolling. Also used as a general term for any roll or throw

Shift (points) To move both men from one point to another, often while hitting a loose blot

Slot To voluntarily place a blot on an important point with a view to making that point if the blot is not hit

Snake Eyes A roll of double ones

Split To move a back man occupying an anchor one or more pips, while remaining in the opponent's home board

Steaming Making irrational cube decisions in money games in a desperate attempt to recover previous losses

Take To accept an offered cube

Timing A measure of how long one can retain a desired position before being forced to make concessions

Trap Play To volunteer a direct shot with a view to forcing the opponent to move off an anchor

Wait To decide not to to double or redouble on this turn

Wash A settlement where two or more players agree that no points will be won by either side in this game. It normally occurs when the chances are approximately equal, and sometimes with a high cube

Weaver To deliberately make an inferior play hoping to get your opponent to accept the cube incorrectly next turn

Bibliography

The following books, in approximate order of difficulty, are recommended reading for anyone wishing to improve:

Backgammon by Paul Magriel

Backgammon for Serious Players by Bill Robertie

Joe Sylvester v Nack Ballard by Kit Woolsey

Philip Marmorstein v Michael Greiner by Kit Woolsey

Mika Lidov v Hal Heinrich by Kit Woolsey

Advanced Backgammon, vol. 1 and 2 by Bill Robertie

New Ideas in Backgammon by Kit Woolsey and Hal Heinrich

How to Play Tournament Backgammon by Kit Woolsey

All should be available from the suppliers listed below.

The Internet

There are a number of servers that offer on-line backgammon where you can play against opponents from all over the world. The three sites the author recommends are as follows:

www.fibs.com – The First Internet Backgammon Server

www.gamesgrid.com – Probably the site used by most top players

www.netgammon.com – Maybe now the largest site

www.vog.ru – The friendliest site with great graphics

The first of these sites is free; the other three sites make an annual charge after a free trial period. Full instructions on joining and software for playing can be found on the sites. Details of clubs and tournaments are also available on the Internet. Many suppliers of equipment, books and software are also listed on the Internet. Two recommended ones are:

Carol Joy Cole, 3719 Greenbrook Lane, Flint, MI 48507-1400 USA; tel/fax: (810) 232 9731; email: cjc@flint.org

Michael Crane, BIBA, 2 Redbourne Drive, Lincoln LN2 2HG; tel: (01522) 888676; email: biba@globalnet.co.uk

Chart for converting score to International Rating

The positions in this book have been tested on a number of players and their scores used to produce a rating chart in which you can look up your score. Total the number of positions you answered correctly and that is your percentage score (give yourself half a mark if you were partly correct or used the hint). Convert it into a rating using the following chart:

%	Rating	%	Rating	%	Rating	%	Rating
100	2100	75	1800	50	1500	25	1200
99	2088	74	1788	49	1488	24	1188
98	2076	73	1776	48	1476	23	1176
97	2064	72	1764	47	1464	22	1164
96	2052	71	1752	46	1452	21	1142
95	2040	70	1740	45	1440	20	1130
94	2028	69	1728	44	1428	19	1128
93	2016	68	1716	43	1416	18	1116
92	2004	67	1704	42	1404	17	1104
91	1992	66	1692	41	1392	16	1092
90	1980	65	1680	40	1380	15	1080
89	1968	64	1668	39	1368	14	1068
88	1956	63	1656	38	1356	13	1056
87	1944	62	1644	37	1344	12	1044
86	1932	61	1632	36	1332	11	1032
85	1920	60	1620	35	1320	10	1020
84	1908	59	1608	34	1308	9	1008
83	1896	58	1596	33	1296	8	996
82	1884	57	1584	32	1284	7	984
81	1872	56	1572	31	1272	6	972
80	1860	55	1560	30	1260	5	960
79	1848	54	1548	29	1248	4	948
78	1836	53	1536	28	1236	3	936
77	1824	52	1524	27	1224	2	924
76	1812	51	1512	26	1212	1	912

To give you a rough idea what these figures mean, the top players in the world are around 2000 including Snowie and Jellyfish, the two strongest computer programs. The average British player is 1500. Someone who has just learnt the game and has been playing a few months would be about 1000. All the Internet servers have rating systems.